BEYOND THE BANKING HOLIDAY

Under The New "Bail In" Banking Rules, Banks Now Own Your Deposits, Not You, What You Can Do About It To Survive & Prosper!

JOHN & MONICA MILLER

Elen Brown, Gerald Celente, Nick Bisley, Mike Adams, The Economic Collapse, King World News, Sovereign Man, Jason Hamlin, Tyler Durden, Doug Casey, Greg Canovan, Bill Holter, Bitreserve, Michael Snyder, Goldseek.com, Jeff Thomas, Callum Newman, David Chapman

Miller & Co.
Auckland

CONTENTS

BEYOND The Banking Holiday!!

This is our sixth book in *"The Coming Series"*, and has to do with further helping Americans protect and build their life savings. In our previous books, we discuss the weakness of the U.S. banking system, including the newly instituted "bail in" program, hyperinflation, expatriation, and protecting one's self by investing in gold. This book is different. It spells out what Global banks intend to do with our savings during the next banking crisis.

Americans, including ourselves, felt that when we put our money in our local bank, the money we put in was ours. Not any more! Once the teller takes your money, and gives you the deposit slip, it becomes *the bank's money*. Chapter one explains the new rules, as of November, 2014, that we must all now live with.

John and Monica Miller are Americans living in Auckland, New Zealand. Besides writing books to help Americans get their investments and savings out of harm's way, they write a weekly newsletter, provide free financial advice, and answer all E-Mails. With regard to this book, the Millers say Americans must quickly learn the new banking rules, and take appropriate measures to protect themselves, and fast!

For those readers, or radio listeners needing some assistance in getting some of your savings out of harm's way, please write us an e-mail at: john@banking-holiday.com, or wallst101@hotmail.com. Monica and I will do our best in answering all your questions and concerns.

There is now, no need for you to travel to NZ

or Australia, to open a savings account, as we originally did. This can all be done for you easily and safely using the Internet. Presently, New Zealand's CD's are paying 3.6% interest (per year), and you only have to hold them for one month (as opposed to 1-5 years in America). As a further safety measure, your CD's are purchased within a "custodian account" (purchasing a "CD" within a custodian account is not available in the U.S.).

Limits of Liability and Disclaimer of Warranty

The author and publisher shall not be liable for your misuse of this material. This book is strictly for informational and educational purposes.

Warning – Disclaimer

The purpose of this book is to educate and entertain. The author and/or publisher do not guarantee that anyone following these techniques, suggestions, tips, ideas, or strategies will become successful. The author and/or publisher shall have neither liability nor responsibility to anyone with respect to any loss or damage caused, or alleged to be caused, directly or indirectly by the information contained in this book.

John & Monica Miller

Waiheke Island, Auckland, New Zealand

Maui, Hawaii

(727) 564 9416 (U.S. Telephone)

http://banking-holiday.com

mailto:john@banking-holiday.com

mailto:wallst101@hotmail.com

Testimonials

"John & Monica were nice enough to give us a pre-published E-Book, and we were flabbergasted to learn that the money we had in the bank, belongs to the bank, not us. Also, we knew nothing about "Bail ins". Why would Americans put their savings in the bank if it were not 100% secure? A great shocking read!" *Phil Thompson, Tampa, Florida*

"This book tells us stuff that we never knew before. Why the FDIC may not be there to safeguard our money. I thought that our savings were insured up to $250,000, and if the bank ran into trouble, we would get reimbursed immediately. After reading, I found out that this is not true, and I might have to wait 15 years to get whole again. How could I pay my mortgage, or feed my family in the interim? Thank you John & Monica for giving us the real scoop!" *John Sawyers, Bayside, New York*

"The book should be read by everyone having money, or investments in the bank. The Millers spell out what our rights are versus the banksters rights, and we come out second. I intend to keep just enough money in my bank account to pay the bills, the rest I will send overseas!" *Susan Collins, New York, New York*

"It's a short, but a powerful book. I had no idea that my money in my local bank was not safe. I intend to spread the word, and try to get my State to start a public bank, and buy some gold and silver now!" *William Scott, Honolulu, Hawaii*

"The Millers other books were great, but this one tells the story concerning how the bankers intend to protect their interests during the next financial collapse, with our money, not theirs". *Betty Saunders, Sante Fe, Mexico*

John Miller is a Graduate of Georgetown University with a Master's Degree In Public Administration. John served as an artillery army *spotter-pilot* during the Viet Nam Era (serving in both Korea & the U.S). After military service, he began his career on Wall Street, working for many of Wall Street's top firms (Dean Witter, Interstate Securities & Lehman Brothers).

After twenty years in the securities business, he started his own investment firm, Miller & Associates. The firm began operations in Florida, and subsequently relocated to Maui, Hawaii. John presently manages Miller & Associates, in Maui, Hawaii, and NZ Trans Global Investments, in Auckland, NZ.

John & his wife Monica moderate of the "Investment Club International. This is an Internet *social, & educational* investment club, with over 2,000 members worldwide, and is free. John writes a weekly newsletter for the club, and does his best to answer questions from the membership. He resides, with his wife Monica in Waiheke Island, New Zealand.

Monica Miller's career involved work as an International sales, marketing, and product development professional, for the Spa & beauty industry. Besides the US, she traveled frequently throughout Asia, and Europe.

Monica was instrumental in forming, and moderating the Maui Investment club. She hosted the popular "Maui" radio talk show: *The Investment Club*. The show's format was similar to the popular "Doland's" radio show.

CHAPTER 1.

AS OF NOVEMBER 2014, THE MONEY IN YOUR BANK ACCOUNT, DOESN'T BELONG TO YOU ANYMORE!

After the economic crisis of 2008, The Financial Stability Board was formed to act as a financial social club of sorts, almost a pseudo legal body that will formulate banking rules into the future.

At the G-20 Summit (November 15-16), 2014, the top twenty nations met to discuss how they could stimulate economic global growth. The World leaders reaffirmed their goal of lifting the GDP of the G-20 economies – which represent 85% of the world's economy – by an additional 2% within four years, by 2018. It's equivalent to adding $2 trillion to global output, and they said that will create millions of jobs.

On the way out of the meeting, all dignitaries were asked to sign an agreement which will pave the way of the new universally accepted "bail in" program. All signed without even looking, so we are told. This signing, without reading, reminds me of the recent omnibus bill passed by congress signed on December 9th, 2014. I'll discuss this bill shortly as it will play a part in the FDIC's alleged safety net.

This new bail in protocol is now considered the law of the land here in the U.S. It is not a treaty, nor was it passed by congress. However, this new procedure will indeed be tested when anyone the of the top six major banks become insolvent. Actually, all of the major banks today are truly insolvent, but when some *black swan* event causes a major to topple due to it's derivatives, the *bail in* plan will be put into motion. For example, Bank Of America has one trillion in deposits, but it's Merrill Lynch division has 50 trillion in derivatives. It wouldn't take much to put Merrill over the edge, thus putting Bank Of America, over the edge.

I should explain exactly what a derivative is before going any further. In simplest form, a derivative is a *bet*. For example, it could be a bet that interest rates will not rise, or oil will remain stable at $100 a barrel. Interest rates have not risen yet, therefore those derivatives issued by the major banks are not presently a concern. However oil has fallen over 50% over the past six months, and is a concern.

Getting back to the congressional omnibus bill mentioned above. Again, at the last moment the administration added a paragraph to the bill concerning derivatives. The addition stated that the government would be responsible to bail out banks possessing derivatives. However, not all derivatives, and this is where the rub comes in. Any *commodity- related* derivative would still remain the bank's liability. How much, in trillions, does this amount to? Fourteen trillion! This is a huge amount, and enough to crater one or all of the major banks, especially if the domino effect takes place.

Looking at Bank of America's 50 trillion derivatives, it is estimated that of the 50 trillion, at least 10 trillion are oil related. Thus if just two trillion of their derivatives have to be paid out by Merrill, it would just be a matter of time, that the Bank Of America would have to shut it's doors. Buy wait, won't the FDIC come to it's rescue (the depositor's rescue)? Yes, and no.

The FDIC insures all bank depositors up to $250,000. This we all know, but what most don't know is that the FDIC has only 46 billion to cover 10 trillion in overall deposits. Therefore, if just one of the major banks went under, the FDIC would be insolvent. However, the FDIC can approach the U.S. treasury, and borrow what it needs. Two problems arise from this. One, this is capital infusion, and has to be paid back to the treasury. For example, if the FDIC borrowed 1 trillion from the treasury, all the banks in America would be assessed. While the top five or six big banks could possibly pay back the loan, and survive, the other 20,000 U.S. banks would close their doors. Perhaps this was the plan all along...

The second problem with borrowing from the treasury is once again related to derivatives. If one major bank fails due to it's inability to pay for it's derivate liability, this would in all probability, cause the other majors to fail (as they are on the other side of the bet). If this occurred, and subsequently, 17 trillion of commodity derivatives came due, even the treasury would not be able to handle.

Let's imagine you are a $250,000 depositor with the Bank Of America. You read in the papers that due to the price of oil falling to $30, Merrill Lynch's derivatives have caused the bank to become insolvent. You visit your branch manager, and he says "bring the matter to the FDIC, as they are handling everything". The FDIC then says that according to the G-20 signing, that they must strictly follow the new *bail in* procedure. They explain it like this. There are now no more *bail outs* by the U.S. government, only *bail ins*. The depositors are considered unsecured creditors of the bank now. The depositors stand behind the secured creditors, and most importantly, behind the *commodity* derivatives.

CHAPTER 2.

THE COMING BANKING HOLIDAY!

"The Fed's behavior over the past 15 months has put America on a very dangerous path. The Fed has increased the monetary base (high-powered or wholesale money) by the largest amount ever, from colonial times to the pres- ent, times 10. Without an exit strategy, inflation is a virtual certainty over the coming decade, while an effective exit strategy virtually assures a further weakening of the US economy. Chairman Bernanke has put the US economy in a lose/lose situation." —Arthur B. Laffer, economist

It's happened before, it can happen again, and it can happen anyway. In America, back in 1933, the government called a "bank holiday" to stop masses of depositors from pulling their money out of the banks. Now, in 2015, in America and around the world there are ominous economic times and the possibility of a repeat run on the banks cannot be dismissed. As conditions deteriorate, particularly in the euro zone, our reiterated forecast for an economic 9/11 striking the equity markets is becoming increasingly plausible. In the event of a financial calamity, will a panicked public start pulling its money out of the markets and out of the banks? In such a scenario, how would governments respond? Would they, as they did back in 1933, make it illegal to own gold coins and gold bullion? Or now, with Big Brother knowing who bought what from whom, and when, would the government seize gold warehouse receipts, raid gold depositories, and, this time, even raid people's homes?

I WANT YOUR GOLD

Would the government force owners of gold to sell it to them at a deep discount price? Employing, verbatim, the language of the Gold Confiscation Act of 1933, Executive Order 6102, when President Franklin D. Roosevelt declared, "by the virtue of the authority vested in me by Section 5(b) of the Act of October 6, 1917..." etc., etc., he essentially decreed, "I'm going to take your gold from you and pay you what I want for it."

In 1933, the government made the people sell their gold to Uncle Sam at $20.57 an ounce. Immediately after the confiscation, the Federal Reserve jacked up the price to $35 an ounce, an increase of nearly 70 percent, thereby devaluing the dollar. It would take $35 in cash to buy what you used to be able to buy with a $20 gold coin. If a bank holiday were called, would ATMs function, and if so, would they be limited to spitting out just a few dollars at a time? Would safety deposit boxes be seized? Would savings and checking accounts be frozen? Bank holiday? Confiscation? Won't happen! Can't happen again! Think Again!

Flashback to 2008, with the economy in tatters, Gerald Celente boldly warned of the strong possibility of a bank holiday being imposed following the inauguration of Barack Obama. He sug- gested that prudent *Trends Journal* subscribers "might consider preparing for such contingencies by having ready access to cash and gold. When banks reopen following a 'holiday,' limits may be set on withdrawal amounts and the currency may have been devalued, officially or de facto."

A bank holiday? Not a remote chance! The prospect was brushed off or ignored by the media. Celente's prediction was made at a time when the majority of the public, as well as the global financial markets, were on an emotional high believing the new President would deliver on campaign promises of "Hope" and "Change You Can Believe In." The best and brightest were on board with Obama, and plans were in place to regenerate the economy. The injection of billions of Fed stimulus dollars would generate millions of shovel-ready "Recovery" jobs and the good times would roll again. In reality, the economic pain and hard- ship that would hit people and businesses after the "Panic of '08" had just begun. As we wrote in 2008 and early 2009 when the first bailouts, rescue plans, Fed money injections, and stimulus plans were announced, they were just "cover-ups" and there would be no "Recovery."

It was all smoke and mirrors, a confidence-building con job designed to make the public believe that recovery was at hand. As we would later learn, Washington's optimistic public face concealed its private awareness of the true nature of the financial damage left in the wake of the Panic.

In fact, the strong possibility of having to call a bank holiday was foremost on the minds of the new Administration. Was the White House reading the *Trends Journal*? Were they listening to Celente's forecast?

As Vice President Joe Biden admitted in June 2009, "Literally one of the early [discussions was] whether we might have to call a bank holiday…a bank holiday on the day after we were sworn in." "A bank holiday?" "A bank holiday on the day after we were sworn in?" Imagine! The entire economic system would come to a virtual standstill. "Holiday?" It would be no holiday and no picnic for the people unable to get their hands on their money. Moving Forward Now, in 2015, the public has lost confidence that world leaders, politicians and technocrats can solve the economic problems they had promised, but failed, to fix.

No longer heard are their encouraging words about sprouting "green shoots." Real world economic conditions have deterio- rated far beyond what they were in 2009. Much of the real estate market has not recovered; those sectors and countries that es- caped serious damage are now weakening, and countries whose housing markets soared are beginning to hear the bubbles burst- ing. Unemployment is as bad as ever, and in many places much worse. Unlike in 2009, when euphoria was still in the air and the ECB chief could, with a straight face, express "confidence that the appropriate decisions will be taken" by the Greek government to resolve its problems, in 2011, those lines were laugh- able. And by 2015, Greece is but a minor problem within a pan- European sovereign debt crisis ...a crisis that was not even taken into consideration back in 2009 when the Obama White House was already contemplating a bank holiday.

With trillions spent, lent and guaranteed by the EMU, ECB and IMF in an unsuccessful attempt to stem the debt crisis, the European financial fiasco has added a troubling dimension to global instability. The prospects for Economic Martial Law have gone commensurately global. Where to put your money, what currency to hold, and who to trust to hold it so that it would not be confiscated or frozen by the government were questions already being asked in 2011. Now, in 2015, the smart money around the world is taking proactive measures, or has plans in place to navigate their cash and themselves to safety in anticipation of a declaration of Economic Martial Law. Capital and wealthy citizens will be flying out of destabilized countries in search of safe havens for their money and/or themselves.

Trendpost: If financial factors alone are not enough to precipitate Economic Martial Law, emergency measures could be en- acted in response to war or a terror strike (false flag or real). If so, will you be able to get your hands on your money in the event of a major attack? Do you remember what happened in the US on 9/11? Wall Street closed, and neither stocks nor CDs could be cashed out until it reopened a week later. Now, with the global economy so fragile and interdependent, a major strike anywhere would cause a financial panic everywhere. Governments could call a bank holiday. Or a cyber attack could sabotage the entire system, making withdrawals impossible.

Publisher's Note: The above bank holiday scenario is how I, as a trend analyst, see Economic Martial Law unfolding. (Gerald Celente)

Courtesy of Gerald Celente's Trends Journal, *Winter*

Our comment: Monica and I have been fans of Gerald Celente for the past 10 years. Our investment club members used to ask us at the end of each meeting: Do you think there will be a "banking holiday" next month? We always answered, "If you have 80% of your net worth in gold and silver, why should you care? Most US investors have zero in gold and silver, and when the banking holiday does occur, you will become rich, almost overnight, vis à vis those that had all their funds in cash at the bank."

Will there really be a banking holiday? It's our opinion that it's a 30% chance of it. Desperate nations do desperate things. Time permitting, the government will attempt to just "print its way out," inflating the national debt. However, if we do have a third world war or a major "event" (such as a 9/11), all bets are off; look for a banking holiday of sorts. The average American will wake up some morning and CNN will announce that all banks will be closed for a period of one week. At the end of this time, a new "red " currency will be available at a 50% conversion rate.

Our action: Starting in 2005, we put all 90% resources into gold and silver, and stored it in Switzerland. We maintained about 10% on hand to cover everyday expenses. We rent our home, we breakfast at the beach each day, we work each night from 2 a.m. to 10 a.m. helping our clients invest in gold and silver shares, and we live each day as it if were a coming banking holiday. Our 500 clients are well aware of this possibility, and we reinforce this with monthly newsletters

CHAPTER 3.

THE "ASIA INFRASTRUCTURE INVESTMENT BANK" FORCASTS THE DEATH OF THE U.S. DOLLAR?

Until last week, the only developed economies to have signed on to China's proposed Asian Infrastructure Investment Bank (AIIB) were Singapore and New Zealand. The choices of those minnows of the global economy were not thought significant as all the major wealthy economies stayed away.

Then, suddenly, Britain announced it was going to sign up as a foundation member. France, Germany and Italy promptly followed.

This rush of support for the China-led initiative resulted in a rather surprising public spat between the US and the UK governments. The two long-term allies have not always agreed with one another but they have normally kept their disagreement from public.

The UK's decision, evidently taken with little consultation with the US, was criticised in surprisingly strident terms. The UK was portrayed as kow-towing to Chinese power.

STRATEGIC POWERPLAY BACKFIRES

The US has for some time sought to keep its allies and friends from supporting the bank and has done so very publicly. Its stated concerns that the AIIB might undermine existing multilateral financial institutions, that it might lower standards in governance and the environment and that its decision-making processes were decidedly opaque are quite reasonable.

The problem is that the US has not been especially constructive in its attitude toward the bank and has not sought to work with China and others to resolve these problems.

The reason for this, many believe, is that lurking not far below these technical concerns about the bank's putative structure and operation is America's real worry: that the bank will allow China greater strategic influence in Asia.

It was these issues that led the Australian government to turn down the invitation to join. The cabinet was reportedly divided on the issue. Trade Minister Andrew Robb and Treasurer Joe Hockey were in favour of joining. Others, led by Foreign Minister Julie Bishop, argued against due to largely strategic concerns.

Now, on the back of the Europeans opting in, Australia looks poised to reverse its initial decision. Briefings and media appearances indicate that Australia is likely to join by the March 31 deadline.

This is not only the latest in a long line of backflips by an Abbott government clearly lacking in policy direction, but it is illustrative of the gravitational force that China is having on world politics.

FORCED TO MAKE A CHOICE

The Australian thinking about China's rise has been dominated by the idea of choice. Prominent scholars and analysts argued that the changing geoeconomic balance meant Australia had to move away from its close alliance with the US to strike a better balance between its interests in the region.

However, governments of both persuasions claimed that Australia did not have to choose between China and the US. Australia's circumstances meant that would did not have to trade off its economic and security interests.

Yet the efforts to create something that, on the face of it, should be uncontroversial – a bank to finance the region's desperate need for infrastructure investment – has shown that hard choices do indeed have to be made. And, as a result, increasingly the US has diplomatic egg on its face as more and more allies and friends opt not to follow its lead.

The policy decision about the AIIB did not have to boil down to the kind of stark choice between China and the US that it has become. The problem is that rather than engaging in a more collaborative and consultative approach, the US very publicly opted to pressure partners to remain aloof. This created precisely the kind of zero-sum decision-making everyone had hoped to avoid.

Even if the diplomacy around the AIIB had been more deft, we cannot ignore that managing the international implications of rising great powers is very difficult. It inevitably involves hard choices.

China is so large, its interests so great and of such global consequence that it simply cannot be stitched into a set of existing international arrangements. More importantly, China has a view of the kind of international order it wants. This plainly does not conform with the views emanating from the US.

The current trajectory of Australian and American policy in Asia is informed by the misguided notion that China can and should conform to the prevailing institutions and structures, and that everyone's interests can be reconciled within the current order. The messy diplomacy around the AIIB's formation shows that this thinking is at best misguided and at worst positively dangerous.

If these latest developments do not prompt some change in both tactics and strategy, the region will change much more quickly and in ways Australia and the US do not like.

Courtesy, by Nick Bisley, The Conversation

CHAPTER 4.

WHY GREECE IS THE LYNCHPIN THAT COULD UNLEASH ECONOMIC COLLAPSE, DOMESTIC MARTIAL LAW AND GLOBAL WAR

I wish I could download to your brain everything you need to know about the European Crisis unfolding right now. The possibility of the breakup of the European Union could be the spark that sets off the **global debt implosion** that leads to violent conflict across the globe.

The actions of Greece, it turns out, could set off a chain reaction that leads directly to a Wall Street panic and the "bail-in" seizure of your savings accounts at your favorite hometown bank. It could also radically destabilize Eastern Europe, heightening the risk for conflict between Russia and Western European nations (including NATO members like the United States).

To understand why this is, we first need to grasp the basics of European history. The average American, unfortunately, knows virtually nothing about European history. But that might be asking too much, since the average American also knows nothing about *American* history, either. Fortunately, this article is written for exceptional Americans who are far better informed than the average Joe.

SOCIALISM KEEPS RUNNING OUT OF OTHER PEOPLE'S MONEY

Greece is bankrupt. Like all socialist states, it has "run out of other people's money," and in this case the "other people" are primarily the German people. Modern-day Germany is the economic miracle of Europe, having risen out of the ashes of World War II, defeated and shamed, to reclaim its role as the single most powerful nation in Europe. What Germany once commanded with its military might, it now commands with its economic miracle machine.

The German people are smart, diligent, innovative and quality-minded. But they've grown weary of bailing out the miserably inefficient government spending of Greece and what they see as a "culture of incompetence and corruption" in that nation. (Can you blame them?) When Germany demanded Greece cut its government spending through austerity programs, the Greek people elected a radical, inexperienced new government into power that declared the austerity cuts to be implausible and refused to play ball with Europe's central bankers.

Right now, Germany and Greece are in a dangerous game of chicken, with Greece saying it won't repay its debt obligations to European banks because those very same central banks functioned as criminals that unfairly exploited the Greek economy through dishonest imperialist debt schemes. Yes, there's a long story here involving

Goldman Sachs, mafia banksters and dastardly financial ploys that crippled Greece's economic future, but that's all too much for this short article.

A GREEK EXIT COULD UNRAVEL A CASCADE OF DEBT

At stake here is the future of the European Union. If Greece pulls out — a scenario now called a "Grexit" — most observers believe the European Union will crumble soon after. To call such an outcome catastrophic is a vast understatement. It could cause a massive global **unwinding of debt-ridden nations and their banks**, potentially leading to a cascading global debt collapse that would very quickly find its way to American shores.

First, as the collapse spread like a virus across Europe, capital would flee to the U.S., causing an unprecedented blowout skyrocketing of U.S. stocks. Soon after, the U.S. stock market would crash hard as even U.S. banks become insolvent due to their exposure to the cascade of European bank failures. (All the globalist banks are fatally intertwined at this point...)

But this isn't even the interesting part yet: Greece is now correctly asserting that Germany has never repaid its war debts to Greek central banks. During the war, the Nazi regime forced the Greek banks to loan it money (at gunpoint, the same way the CDC wants to force Americans to take vaccine shots). These loans accrued over many decades, never being repaid. Instead of repaying the debt, Germany's politicians have attempted to memory hole the issue, pretending that fundamental principles of debt and accounting don't apply wherever the political elite say they don't. But according to this extraordinary article in Der Spiegel, "The commission calculated the outstanding German 'debt' to the Greek central bank and came to a total sum of $12.8 billion as of December 2014."

Germany, in other words, owes Greece $12.8 billion on a debt dating back to the era of Adolf Hitler. Greece is now demanding repayment of this debt as an implied condition of it staying in the European Union. $12.8 billion isn't pocket change. Not even for Germany. And the willingness of the

German people to keep funneling money to Greece is rapidly eroding.

Beyond that, there's also the issue of a few hundred million dollars worth of gold stolen by the Third Reich. As Der Spiegel reports:

Karakousis spent five months reading 50,000 pages of original documents from the central bank's archives. It wasn't easy reading. The study calculates right down to the gram the amount of gold plundered from private households, especially those of Greek Jews: 7,358.0014 kilograms of pure gold with an equivalent value today of around [$250 million].

It seems the Greeks want their gold back... or at least a currency equivalent of all the gold that was stolen from them. And now this has become an issue with huge implications for the future of the world.

Why does any of this matter, you say?

A COLLAPSE OF THE EUROPEAN UNION WOULD CATASTROPHICALLY DESTABILIZE ALL OF EUROPE

What most Americans don't realize is that **Europeans have very long memories of crimes against their people**. These memories are passed down from generation to generation and can't simply be greenwashed out of the history books.

The European Union was formed on the hope and assumption that people from an incredibly diverse array of cultural backgrounds might forgive the past and surrender to cultural homogenization as "Europeans." But the hope turned out to be false. The people of Greece in 2015 still remember the crimes of Nazi Germany from 1943, even long after they have been officially absorbed into the European Union. And now that memory may very well result in the shattering of the European Union itself.

If the European Union crumbles, **Europe will see a wave of regional wars** breaking out over so-called "borderlands" and strategic nations like Ukraine. The fall of the European Union, in fact, would likely embolden Russia to be even more assertive in the Ukraine as it attempts to defend itself from America's ever-encroaching military bases which now occupy most of Russia's border states. (Why did Putin put his country so darn close to all our military bases? Geesh…)

Russia, you see, must maintain strategic control over these border states in order to export its primary resource: energy. Germany, meanwhile, must maintain strong economic ties with wealthy nations that can afford to import Germany's high cost value added exports — the backbone of the German economy. A shattering of the European Union would destabilize both Germany and Russia for these two reasons (exports of energy and exports of manufactured goods), reigniting the same sort of fears and insecurities that drove the German invasion of Russia in World War II. That invasion was a strategic move to occupy Stalingrad not for the city itself, but because the city was a gateway to the enormous energy and strategic resources of Mother Russia, which Hitler needed to fuel his thirsty war machine.

NATO AND GERMANY ARE MILITARILY WEAK

Today, Germany has no military to speak of. Russia, on the other hand, is re-emerging as a very powerful military force with considerable leverage throughout Western Europe due to its energy pipelines. NATO, meanwhile, exists in name only and is primarily backed by the threat of military force from America, a nation bogged down in endless (and pointless) military action in the Middle East.

While America was defusing roadside bombs in Afghanistan, Russia was busy occupying the "strategic high ground" of the North Pole, as described in this article by Dave Hodges. This places Russia in a position where it can credibly threaten all of Western Europe and North America with nuclear strikes (if it ever comes to that).

Russia, too, is populated by strong, rugged, durable people who are used to surviving with little in the way of material goods. They can endure war far more readily than wealthy, pampered nations like America or the UK. As a matter of record, young Americans are now so obese that even the U.S. military must reject almost a quarter of all applicants due to excessive body weight.

ECONOMIC WARFARE WILL LIKELY PRECEDE MILITARY WARFARE

On the economic side, Russia has joined forces with China to erect its own alternative to the SWIFT inter-bank money transfer system. China has been accumulating a massive amount of gold reserves to back its currency, while Russia has been selling off the U.S. dollar and bypassing western sanctions in creative ways by selling energy in exchange for physical gold.

The dollar itself is headed for a global collapse for the simple reason that it isn't backed by anything other than (dwindling) faith. President Nixon removed the gold backing of the dollar in 1971, and ever since, America has been headed toward a day of reckoning where the dollar would eventually collapse as all fiat currencies do. Faith in the dollar is eroding by the day as the Fed keeps printing more money, diluting the existing money supply and silently stealing wealth from those people foolish enough to still be holding dollars when the music stops (i.e. all U.S. wage earners and taxpayers). Fort Knox, meanwhile, isn't filled with gold but rather IOUs. Most of the physical gold has been quietly but diligently accumulated by China over the last two decades.

THE STAGE IS NOW SET FOR A GLOBAL ECONOMIC WAR AIMED AT AMERICA AND THE DOLLAR HEGEMONY

I'm barely touching the highlights of the global dynamics at play here, but what's really taking shape is a global economic and military war, waged by China and Russia against the Western powers of the United States, NATO, the European Union and Germany in particular. Greece now plays the role of the lynchpin in all this, as its exit from the European Union could loosen the knot that unravels the empire of debt upon which

Western nations are now based. An economic implosion leads to systemic weakness which invites more aggressive economic warfare actions on the part of Russia and China.

If a combined economic action by Russia and China were to take place — for example, China announcing a fire sale of U.S. debt while Russia cuts off energy supplies to Western Europe — the economic implications for Europe and America would be beyond catastrophic. They might be terminal. We would see the U.S. government, for example, instantly unable to sell any new debt to foreign nations. The only option is to print more money to finance the debt — a form of economic suicide — and with the loss of the dollar's global currency reserve status, this would lead very quickly to accelerating money debasement and price hyperinflation in consumer goods. Think Venezuela: price controls, biometric scanning requirements to purchase groceries. Armed guards at grocery stores. Food shortages, street riots, etc.

It wouldn't be long before the U.S. government would be forced to stop funding entitlement programs such as EBT cards and pensions. This would almost immediately lead to massive riots in the streets and the wholesale destruction of large cities such as St. Louis and Chicago. From here, it gets even uglier with declarations of Martial Law, the suspension of the Bill of Rights, and the military occupation of America's cities in order to maintain order.

The problem with all entitlement-based Western nations (including America) is that sooner or later you run out of other people's money. When that day of reckoning comes, the population that has come to depend on entitlements for day-to-day existence finds itself abandoned by the very government that promised to take care of them. Chaos ensues.

This all explains why Germany and the United States are desperate to prevent the breakup of the European Union and the continued illusion of economic stability. As Germany is now discovering to its horror, the problem with debt is that **sooner or later you have to repay it**. But all the Western governments of the world have accrued far more debt than they can ever repay, and the collapse of the European Union would savagely reveal those debts.

If there's one thing America, the UK and the European Union cannot handle right now, it's **debt transparency**. The day the truth about debt and spending becomes widely acknowledged, faith in the dollar collapses and the world nosedives into a tailspin. Watch Greece carefully, for your own future depends strongly on what happens there.

Courtesy, Mike Adams, the Health Ranger

CHAPTER 5.

33 STRANGE FACTS ABOUT AMERICA THAT MOST AMERICANS WOULD BE SHOCKED TO LEARN!

Did you know that about one-fourth of the entire global prison population is in the United States? Did you know that Apple has more money than the U.S. Treasury? Did you know that if you have no debt and also have 10 dollars in your wallet that you are wealthier than 25 percent of all Americans? Did you know that by the time an American child reaches the age of 18, that child will have seen approximately 40,000 murders on television?

There are some things that are great about the

United States, and there are definitely some things that are not so great. Once upon a time we were the most loved and most respected nation on the entire planet, but those days are long gone. We have wrecked our economy, we have lost our values and we have fumbled away our future. But if you look close enough, you can still see many of the things that once made this country a shining beacon to the rest of the world.

This article includes some weird facts, some fun facts, but also some very troubling facts. It has been said that a spoonful of sugar helps the medicine go down, and hopefully as people enjoy reading the fun facts in this article they will also take note of the more serious facts.

If we are ever going to change course as a nation, we need to come to grips with just how far we have fallen. The following are 33 strange facts about America that most Americans would be shocked to learn...

#1 The amount of cement that China used from 2011 to 2013 was greater than the total amount of cement that the United States used during the entire 20th century.

#2 In more than half of all U.S. states, the highest paid public employee in the state is a football coach.

#3 It costs the U.S. government 1.8 cents to mint a penny and 9.4 cents to mint a nickel.

#4 Almost half of all Americans (47 percent) do not put a single penny out of their paychecks into savings.

#5 In 2014, police in the United States killed 1,100 people. During that same year, police in Canada killed 14 people, police in China killed 12 people and police in Germany didn't kill anyone at all.

#6 The state of Alaska is 429 times larger than the state of Rhode Island is. But Rhode Island has a significantly larger population than Alaska does.

#7 Alaska has a longer coastline than all of the other 49 U.S. states put together.

#8 The city of Juneau, Alaska is about 3,000 square miles in size. It is actually larger than the entire state of Delaware.

#9 When LBJ's "War on Poverty" began, less than 10 percent of all U.S. children were growing up in single parent households. Today, that number has skyrocketed to 33 percent.

#10 In 1950, less than 5 percent of all babies

in America were born to unmarried parents. Today, that number is over 40 percent.

#11 The poverty rate for households that are led by a married couple is 6.8 percent. For households that are led by a female single parent, the poverty rate is 37.1 percent.

#12 In 2013, women earned 60 percent of all bachelor's degrees that were awarded that year in the United States.

#13 According to the CDC, 34.6 percent of all men in the U.S. are obese at this point.

#14 The average supermarket in the United States wastes about 3,000 pounds of food each year.

#15 Right now, more than 200 million people around the planet are officially considered to be unemployed. Meanwhile, approximately 20 percent of the garbage that goes into our landfills is food.

#16 There is a city in Bangladesh called Dhaka where workers are paid just one dollar for every 1,000 bricks that they carry. Meanwhile, the "inactivity rate" for men in their prime working years in the United States is hovering near record high levels.

#17 According to one recent survey, 81 percent of Russians now have a negative view of the United States. That is much higher than at the end of the Cold War era.

#18 Montana has three times as many cows as it does people.

#19 The grizzly bear is the official state animal of California. But no grizzly bears have been seen there since 1922.

#20 One recent survey discovered that "a steady job" is the number one thing that American women are looking for in a husband, and another survey discovered that 75 percent of women would have a serious problem dating an unemployed man.

#21 According to a study conducted by economist Carl Benedikt Frey and engineer Michael Osborne, 47 percent of the jobs in the United States could soon be lost to computers, robots and other forms of technology.

#22 The only place in the United States where coffee is grown commercially is in Hawaii.

#23 The original name of the city of Atlanta was "Terminus".

#24 The state with the most millionaires per capita is Maryland.

#25 There are more than 4 million adult websites on the Internet, and they get more traffic than Netflix, Amazon and Twitter combined.

#26 86 percent of men include "having children" in their definition of success. For women, that number is only 73 percent.

#27 One survey of 50-year-old men in the U.S. found that only 12 percent of them said that they were "very happy".

#28 The United States has 845 motor vehicles for every 1,000 people. Japan only has 593 for every 1,000 people, and Germany only has 540 for every 1,000 people.

#29 The average American spends more than 10 hours a day using an electronic device.

#30 48 percent of all Americans do not have any emergency supplies in their homes whatsoever.

#31 There are three towns in the United States that have the name "Santa Claus".

#32 There is actually a town in Michigan called "Hell".

#33 There are 60,000 miles of blood vessels

in your body. If they were stretched out in a single line, they could go around the planet more than twice.

Courtesy, The Economic Collapse

CHAPTER 6.

THE UNITED STATES, WEIMAR GERMANY AND WHAT THE FED IS REALLY UP TO

Today one of the greats in the business spoke with King World News about the United States, Weimar Germany and what the Fed is really up to. He also included two fantastic illustrations that all KWN readers around the world must see.

James Turk: "Each week the world's financial picture goes further and further into la-la land, Eric. In short, things are getting crazier. An example is the hullabaloo the Federal Reserve created by dropping the word "patience" from its statement after the latest FOMC meeting. The Fed calls these statements 'guidance'. In another era, they would be recognized for what they really are – propaganda….

"The Fed makes these announcements to massage financial markets into doing what the Fed wants them to do. Oddly, it's working. Not only is the Fed rigging markets with its interventions, it's directing markets by its regular announcements. So the distortions in the markets as well as the economy are becoming even greater.

Will The Fed Really Develop A Happy Outcome?

Momentum players dominate the stock

market today, meaning that fewer and fewer investors focus on value anymore. That is leading to trouble because this growing number of investors simply believe that the Fed will develop a happy outcome.

This legion of investors, whether wittingly or not, is ignoring the Fed's track record. They even ignore the details of what the Fed is saying.

In the fine print in this latest announcement, the Fed clearly lowered its outlook for the US economy. That's why oil is still under $50 a barrel. Energy consumption is down because economic activity is weak. Things like gasoline sales continue in the downtrend that began at the peak before the 2008 collapse, as shown on the following chart.

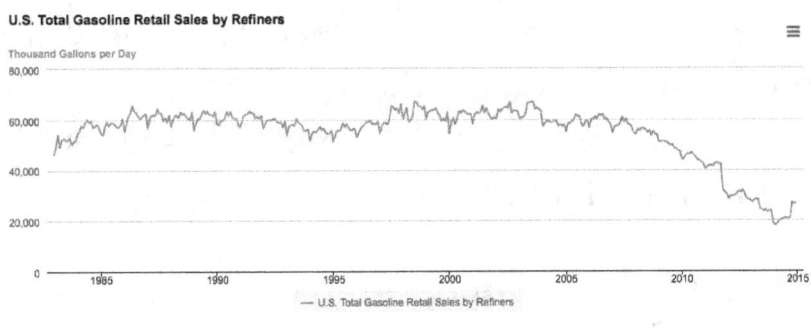

U.S. Total Gasoline Retail Sales by Refiners

Thousand Gallons per Day

— U.S. Total Gasoline Retail Sales by Refiners

eia Source: U.S. Energy Information Administration

So even though the economy is doing worse than the Fed expected, the Fed is still singing the same song. It wants interest rates to stay near zero. The time frame for zero interest rates is now approaching seven years as we can see in the following chart.

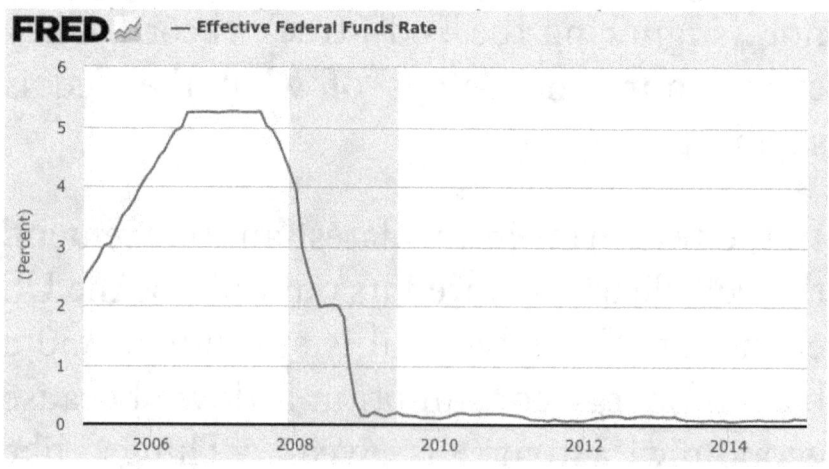

Despite all the evidence that these low interest rates are not helping the economy, the Fed is determined to keep rates low in order to try proving its theories. There are too many PhD's on the line for the Fed to change course, and the country's savers are not a unified force.

So here's the important conclusion to be drawn from this, Eric: Even though the economy is headed into the dumpster, the stock market is headed higher for another reason. The stock boom is a result of Fed mismanagement, just like the speculative stock market booms in 1929 and 1999. We are in an environment where the Fed is killing savers to keep in the air an unsustainable system of borrowing and spending.

The Weimar Comparison

However, this time the outcome may be different from 1929 and 1999. It will be more like the outcome of Weimar Germany, Zimbabwe or any other country that had more debt than the economy could carry. In these countries the currency collapsed.

When a currency collapses, the share price of companies that own tangible assets like agribusinesses, oil companies and miners, continue to climb. These are a safe haven of sorts. However, physical gold and silver have track records that date back thousands of years, proving they are the ultimate safe havens."

Courtesy, King World News

CHAPTER 7.

SIGNS THAT AMERICA WILL HIT THE WALL AND GO SPLAT!!

Disclaimer: The following will happen if and only if we do not arrest the Bankers, seize their assets and have Debt Cancellation combined with monetary and banking reforms.

The US is losing friends and influence as people overseas can see the End is Nigh for the Dollar and for Washington. The Vietnamese are allowing Russians to use former American air bases to fuel long range bombers. And the British have joined China's Asian Infrastructure Investment Bank. The Chinese are trying to push the US out of Asia just as the US pushed Europeans out of Latin America with its Monroe Doctrine in the early 19th century.

Britain, Australia, Germany and other key allies have set up financial hubs to allow direct currency exchanges between their currency and the yuan. The Chinese yuan is the fifth most traded currency in the world.

The BRICS Post said the Chinese are in direct talks with the IMF to include the yuan in the basket of currencies that make up the SDR (Special Drawing Rights.) The four current SDR currencies are the US dollar, the pound, the euro and the Japanese yen. The deadline for inclusion is September 15th this year. The next opportunity for admission will be in 2020. The Obama admin rather arrogantly rebuffed China's last application in 2010.

The Chinese will have to open their gold vaults to public inspection and audit before they can be accepted. Some time this summer we could see just how much gold they have in their vaults. Dr Jim Willie has a source who has worked in Europe helping to sell one thousand tons of gold every month for 30 months from Europe to Asia. That same source and others have said that bullion banks have been stealing gold from European and Arab customers that had been on deposit and selling it to Asians.

The bullion banks have been leasing gold from the Central Banks and the Federal Reserve which they sell five times as paper certificates of gold on deposit. Some of those banks have had to refuse to redeem their gold deposits. And recently the Bank of England told the Austrians that their gold might have disappeared.

Jim Rickards, a CIA and DOD monetary adviser, said he has talked to a man who brought gold into China that was never listed on any official observer's website. China has been buying gold mines. It will be interesting to see the Chinese open their vaults to inspection.

The euro has dropped to a 12 year low of $1.05. The Greeks were told that they should stop paying wages and pensions for a month or two so they would have enough money to make their loan payment to the Banks. Obviously, Bankers have never tried to work as a hospital orderly or drove a truck. Only sheltered people could think that workers would show up to their job and be willing to forget paydays for the next two months.

The US dollar is currently surging in exchange value because investors and speculators are buying trillions of dollars to liquidate losing investments and loans denominated in dollars. The value of a currency is determined by supply and demand. The US since NAFTA does not make things other countries buy. NAFTA closed 57,000 factories and sent 12 million jobs overseas. The US has allowed Monsanto to produce crops which are banned in many nations. America has forced debtor nations in Africa to take Monsanto seeds despite their objections that GMO franken food and their Round Up pesticide will seriously harm the health of the people and the farm animals who eat them.

Once this flurry of loan liquidations is over the dollar should begin to slide. That will be about the time the Chinese open their gold vaults. I do not think the Chinese will immediately announce a gold backed yuan but will first allow the price of gold to rocket towards the heavens in price. That will seriously harm Washington's standing in the world paving the way for the yuan's acceptance into the IMF's SDR basket of currencies.

Hint 1: Any sudden price rise in gold will take silver with it.

Hint 2: The Hong Kong Exchange halted all

gold futures contracts today (Friday the 13th) because the London gold price fix will soon end and be replaced by a Chinese based electronic gold auction. This will be an auction where you have to actually deliver the gold you sold and you are not allowed to sell the bullion you stole from a depositor. HSBC used to be the custodian for the GLD paper gold trust. They closed all of their gold vaults. Good luck getting gold when you sell your GLD shares.

The Federal Reserve is pumping up the value of stocks in New York. They loan dollars at low, near zero interest rates so corporations can buy their own stocks. This makes stock prices rise despite the drop both in earnings per share and in dividends. Poor earnings, declining sales and an increasing debt load will eventually make those stocks look extremely unattractive. But before that day arrives executives can get 'performance based' bonuses and cash in their stock options. Insiders are selling record amounts of stocks in High Tech.

Foreigners are also buying dollars so they can

get into the New York stock market before it collapses. This will not last long. The Baltic Dry Index is down to new lows which means there will be no recovery in production in the near future. And lumber prices and futures have also reached new lows so housing will continue to slump.

The European stock markets are up but nowhere near as much as gold is in foreign currencies. European stocks went up because their Central Bank under Mario Draghi has promised to print a trillion euros. After the stocks have risen in euros, the risk to investors will be that their euro denominated investments will decline in relation to the dollar, to gold and to the yuan.

The Japanese yen is one of those four SDR currencies. Currently, the Japanese debt is one quadrillion yen ($10.46 trillion US). The Japanese government plans to spend 43% of its revenue this year to service the debt. This is not good.

There is also a major risk to the Banks and to the West coming from Credit Default Swaps.

CDS were invented by Blythe Masters of J P Morgan in 1995. What a CDS does is to allow a bank to use their assets to earn revenue without real risk. They give out false insurance guarantees that if the price of oil or a currency like the euro drops below a certain value, they will be paid for the loss.

The Too Big To Jail Bankers sit on the board that determines if your CDS should be paid out. They are very stingy. So why would you buy a CDS? You need one to commit fraud. Pension funds are only allowed to buy AAA rated bonds. When the Banks created trillions of dollars in fraudulent Mortgage Backed Securities, they needed to buy CDS to guarantee them so their worthless securities could receive AAA ratings from agencies that were paid for ratings they did not deserve.

The Federal Reserve saw the handwriting on the wall. A couple of years ago they told the Big Banks to write living wills. That meant they were to separate their assets into several different corporate names. All the good stuff was set aside to survive the coming collapse in the hands of very special people. All the vulnerable assets remained in the commercial bank. All CDS swaps (numbering in hundreds of trillions of dollars) were transferred over to the commercial bank.

The Federal Reserve, the Bank of England and other Central Banks all agreed that bank depositors were to now to be considered as investors in the bank. This means the Bank's creditors could seize the money the depositors had been saving for a rainy day. For example, a man who sold mortgage bonds he knew were to fail could collect on a CDS he bought for pennies on the dollar. He is worthy to be paid from the depositors' savings.

Mark Twain said America has the best Congress money can buy.

The Congress passed a law in December which Obama signed holding US taxpayers liable for the losses the Banks will have on their two hundred trillion plus dollars in potential CDS losses.

Hint 3: The Federal Reserve will never raise

interest rates before the Dollar Dies. The US could never survive an interest rate increase. There are hundreds of trillions of dollars in CDS guarantees on the value of the dollar and against any rise in interest rates.

America and Great Britain are weighed down heavily by corruption.

A Depression is a period in time when Unpayable Debts are canceled en masse. The British have even more Unpayable Debts than the Americans so their forthcoming Depression will be exceedingly severe. The US in for even harder times than they were back in the 1930s when 3 million Americans starved to death because we have more debts now than last time.

There are two events scheduled for September of 2015 that were heavily promoted by Israeli intelligence. I wrote about one recently. It is the Shemitah which is the time when debts were to be cancelled in ancient Israel. It is called the Jubilee in the Bible. It has been presented in the modern media as God pouring his wrath upon

America because of abortion or Gay rights or fill in the blank. It actually is the consequence of a failure to cancel bad debts and has nothing to do with God's Judgement. The Shemitah is scheduled for September 13, 2015 which is a Sunday.

The second event heavily promoted by Israeli intelligence are the four Blood Moons. A rare event that occurs once every 500 years. The fourth and final Blood Moon is to occur on September 28, 2015. It is said to be a sign of war and doom.

September looks like as good a time as any for America to hit a Brick Wall. The Israelis have already prepared prophecies for the gullible to explain why these disasters have nothing to do with banking, the greed of Wall Street and the corruption of the City of London.

I opened with a disclaimer. We need Debt Cancellation and currency reform to prevent these disasters. I wrote about issuing a Debt Free currency and banning fractional reserve banking here:

IMF Economists: 'We Were Wrong.' Will Someone Please Tell The Press And The Politicians.

Courtesy, Jason Hamlin

CHAPTER 8.

GERALD CELENTE – THIS IS GOING TO RADICALLY CHANGE THE WORLD

On a day where stocks are dipping, today the top trends forecaster in the world spoke with King World News about a developing situation that is going to radically change the world in which we live.

Gerald Celente: "Look at what's happening with the Asian Infrastructure Investment Bank (AIIB). Of course when the United Kingdom said they were going to join it, there was a lot of pressure from the United States for them not to join it and yet they did anyway. There are now 35 initial members and it's ready to launch.

So it will be official by next Tuesday, March 31st. This AIIB is going to be a competitor to the IMF and the World Bank. Again, the United States has been putting pressure on its allies not to join but one by one they are joining anyway.

More Countries Continue Joining AIIB

So after the UK, we had France, Germany and Italy join. Now it appears that even South Korea is going to join. When you look at the reasons why these countries are joining it's very clear: The United States has a military pivot to Asia, but China's pivot to Asia is business. So the business of America is war but the business of China is business.

For example, 12 percent of South Korea's exports go to the United States but 25 percent go to China. You can see South Korea's motivation — it's money. So the United States sent over U.S. Assistant Secretary of State, Daniel Russell, to try to talk the South Koreans out of joining. The U.S. was saying they have to make sure the AIIB meets, 'The high-water mark,' of the World Bank and the IMF.

What a bunch of hypocrisy that is because when you look at the people who ran, or are running, the World Bank, one of them was Paul Wolfowitz, the architect of the Iraq War and the Wolfowitz Doctrine that essentially launched an attack against the former Soviet Union, once it collapsed:

"Our first objective is to prevent the re-emergence of a new rival, either on the territory of the former Soviet Union or elsewhere, that poses a threat on the order of that posed formerly by the Soviet Union. This is a dominant consideration underlying the new regional defense strategy and requires that we endeavor to prevent any hostile power from dominating a region whose resources would, under consolidated control, be sufficient to generate global power."

So that's who is running the World Bank. Is that the 'high-water mark' the U.S. demands AIIB sink to?

China Invests In Growth

Then you look at the new president of Afghanistan — he worked for the World Bank for several years. So what's this 'high-water mark?' When you look at the name of it, the Asian Infrastructure Investment Bank, it's anathema to what America does. Over the last 20 years China has invested some 8.5 percent of its GDP annually into infrastructure. And during that same period, the United States' infrastructure investment was a big 0.06 percent.

China Going For The Gold As Western Mainstream Media Silent

So infrastructure and investment are not the kinds of policies America really has much knowledge of. The bottom line is about money. It's the Golden Rule: 'Those who have the gold, rule.' China is going for the gold in their investments into Asia and emerging and developing markets. China is building the Asian economies rather than getting involved in wars.

When you look at the development of the BRIC nations as well, going with their banking systems, you can see this is more and more of a move away from the United States and the dollar as a reserve currency and the United States as a world power. It's a new millennium shift to the East that's being overlooked by the mainstream media, but the implications of this are enormous." ***ALSO RELEASED: Worldwide Markets To See Total Panic As Massive Derivatives Bubble Implodes!

Courtesy, Gerald Celente, and King World News, KingWorldNews.com

CHAPTER 9.

AUSTRALIA TO START TAXING BANK DEPOSITS

Up until now, the world's descent into the NIRPy twilight of fiat currency was a function of failing monetary policy around the globe as central bank after desperate central bank implemented negative and even more negative (in the case of Denmark some four times rapid succession) rates, hoping to make saving so prohibitive consumers would have no choice but to spend the fruits of their labor, or better yet, take out massive loans which they would never be able to repay. However, nobody said it was only central banks who could be the executioners of the world's saver class: governments are perfectly capable too. Such as Australia's.

According to Australia's ABC News, the **"Federal Government looks set to introduce a tax on bank deposits in the May budget."**

Ironically, the idea of a bank deposit tax was raised by Labor in 2013 and was criticized by Tony Abbott at the time. Much has changed in two years, and as ABC reports, assistant Treasurer Josh Frydenberg has indicated an announcement on the new tax could be made before the budget.

Mr Frydenberg is a member of the Government's Expenditure Review Committee but has refused to provide any details.

"Any announcements or decisions around this proposed policy which we discussed at the last election will be made in the lead up or on budget night," he said.

Speaking at the Victorian Liberal State Council meeting Mr Abbott has repeated his budget message, focusing on families and small businesses.

"There will be tough decisions in this year's

budget as there must be, but there will also be good news."

For the banks and creditors, yes. For anyone who is still naive enough to save money in the hopes of deferring purchases for the future, not so much.

The banking industry has raised concerns about a deposit tax, saying it will have to pass the cost back onto customers.

Steven Munchenberg from the Australian Bankers' Association said it would be a damaging move for the Government.

"It's going to make it harder for banks to raise deposits which are an important way of funding banks. And therefore for us to fund the economy," he said. "And we also oppose it because particularly at this point in time with low interest rates **a lot of people who are relying on their savings for their incomes are already seeing very low returns and this will actually mean they get even less money."**

Don't worry Steven, neither central banks

nor government care about "a lot of people" – they just care about a select few. As for the banks, once China, and immediately thereafter Australia, launches QE as the entire world descends into a monetary supernova, and Australia's banks are flooded with trillions in excess reserves like those in the US, all shall be forgiven. As a reminder, banks such as JPM are so flush with zero-cost cash from other sources, well *one* other source, they are now actively turning away depositors.

As for Australia, while central banks are untouchable and unaccountable to anyone (except their commercial bank directors and anyone else they secretly meet during those bimonthly sessions in the BIS tower in Basel), the government can be voted in and voted out. Especially a government that is about to break one of its main election promises:

The Federal Opposition has accused the Government of breaking an election promise by planning to introduce a tax on bank deposits.

The former Labor Government put forward the policy in 2013 to raise revenue for a fund to protect customers in the event of a banking collapse.

Shadow Assistant Treasurer Andrew Leigh said Treasurer Joe Hockey criticised the proposal at the time. "When we put it on the table Joe Hockey said that it was a smash and grab on Australian households just aimed at repairing the budget," he said.

It is almost surprising, but not really, how when it comes down to money, the thin white line between "us" and "them" always disappears when the money runs out.

As for Australia's savers, welcome to the *NIRP world* where savers in increasingly more countries are now on the endangered species list.

Courtesy, Tyler Durden

CHAPTER 10.

BANKS WILL SOON BE CHARGING YOU TO KEEP YOUR MONEY IN THEIR BANK!

Several months ago, the government of Australia proposed to tax bank deposits up to $250,000 at a rate of 0.05% (5 basis points). Their idea was for the money to be invested in a rainy day Financial Stabilization Fund to insure against in the unlikely event of a banking crisis… or all-out collapse.

And as of this morning, it looks like the levy might just pass and become law in Australia. All parties support the idea. Which means that Australia might just have a tax on bank deposits starting January 1, 2016.

To be clear, the proposal seems to plan on

taxing the *banks* based on the amount of deposits they're holding—but it's pretty obvious this will be passed on to consumers in the form of lower interest rates. Let's look at what this means:

1. **Taxes on bank deposits are generally the same as negative interest rates.**Australia is a rare exception. Interest rates on bank deposits in most developed nations are practically zero… if not already negative. So charging a tax above and beyond this would clearly push rates (further) into negative territory. I have, for example, a small bank account in the United States that pays me about .03% interest (three basis points). If the government imposes a tax of 5bp on interest of 3bp, I'm left with negative interest. Australia (along with New Zealand) is a rare exception since interest rates are actually positive. You can get 2-3% on a savings account. So a 5bp tax still results in positive interest.

2. Taxes always start small... then increase over time.

Of course, the proposal on the table right now is a 5bp tax. There's nothing that says this can't increase to 50bp over time. When the United States government first imposed the modern federal income tax a century ago, the top tax rate was just 7%. These days that would qualify the US as a tax haven.

Over time, tax rates rose to as high as 92%. Tax rates can (and do) rise. And once they're passed, they're almost never abolished.

3. Taxes are rarely used for their stated purpose

Politicians create and raise taxes all the time for special purposes. And again, over time, they are often diverted away from those purposes. In 1936 after a devastating flood in Johnstown, Pennsylvania, the state government passed a 'temporary' 10% tax on all alcohol sold in the state in order to help pay for disaster relief. Six years later the work was complete. But the tax is still on the books (now at 18%), with all the revenue going to whatever the state lawmakers want to blow it on.

FICA is another great example.

Though payroll taxes in the US were initially established to fund Social Security and Medicare, the federal government steals this revenue every year to haplessly try and plug budget deficits. So a tax to build a financial stabilization fund might sound comforting in theory... but will all the revenue actually be allocated for that purpose? Doubtful.

4. **If this can happen in Australia, is anyone foolish enough to think it can't happen in the US or Europe?**

Australia has a sound and sturdy banking system. Banks in Australia are actually, you know, solvent. Capital ratios and liquidity rates are solid. Australia's is a well-capitalized banking system—far more than in the US and Europe. The numbers tell a very clear story. Banking systems across Europe in particular have had to be routinely bailed out over the past few years—Slovenia, Spain, Greece, Cyprus, etc.

In the United States it is perhaps even more absurd. Based on their own numbers, US banks are highly illiquid, still gambling away customer funds in trendy investment fads that will likely suffer an epic meltdown. Backing up this little scam is the FDIC, which itself is pitifully under-capitalized to support any significant problem in the banking system. Backing up the FDIC is the US federal government, which is already drowning in more than $60 trillion in liabilities (based on the most recent GAO report). And supplying crack to the crack head is the US Federal Reserve, America's central bank.

With net capital just 1.26% of total assets, the Fed is so pitifully capitalized they make

Lehman Brothers look like Berkshire Hathaway.

So if the government of Australia is concerned that their well-capitalized banking system needs a safety net and wants to tax deposits for such purpose, how in the world can we possibly expect the US and Europe, with all of their banking system risk, won't do the same?

Courtesy, Simon Black, Sovereign Man

CHAPTER 11.

HOW LONG CAN THIS GO ON?

I've received a couple of interesting emails this week that I thought would be worth sharing. You probably have similar concerns.

–Here's the first question:

I like what you have to say and write and agree with your comments most of the time. My email is one of frustration...

While all pundits including Gerald Celente, Marc Faber and to a large extent most of your company's seminars predict a massive financial correction I cannot understand why things like stocks and property keep going up and up globally.

All the fundaments don't make sense. Economic

reasoning doesn't apply any more. Interest rates are so low it's not worth holding cash.

My question is, how much longer do you think this nonsense economy can go on for?

Are we seeing the beginning of a global economic monopoly table (bankers rule everything through sophisticated software) where financial/govt/ economic manipulation is here to stay and the death of economic realities of the market are now long lost and buried?

Are things really getting better? Or are we realists just in one big mental daze assuming foolishly that things are going to get much worse sometime soon. I simply just don't get it. Since 2008 I have waited for a correction to cleanse the system but it looks very unlikely for the next 10 + years.

I would welcome your comment very much.

–That's a big question. I'll attempt a succinct answer.

–The correction in 2008 <u>was</u> an attempt to cleanse the system. But the powers that be decided not to let it run its course. A study released by McKinsey and Co a few months ago showed that, since 2008, global debt levels have increased by US$57 trillion.

–That's the price we've paid to prop up the financial system. And it's still going. The system feeds on an ever expanding pile of debt. That's why you're seeing QE programs running in Japan and now Europe, and it's why the US will never be able to 'normalise' interest rates.

–Central bankers and politicians love to say things are getting better. But they're not. We're merely throwing more debt at a problem that was ultimately caused by too much debt in the first place.

–This masks the underlying problems. The flipside of the explosion of debt is an explosion of asset prices. People mistake this 'wealth' for real economic progress. It's simply inflation expressing itself in another way.

–This is what QE and near zero interest rates do. They inflate asset prices but the stimulus doesn't make its way into the real economy...so there is no inflation in the traditional way we measure it — via consumer goods and services prices.

–Which is insane. You've got the RBA tracking the price of a litre of milk or a loaf of bread very closely because they want to make sure 'the cost of living' doesn't get out of hand. But they are oblivious to the fact that the biggest component in the cost of living — the cost to buy a house — climbs higher and higher.

–To cover this cost, households have to cut back on spending elsewhere, creating less demand for other goods and services, which leads to, OMG, deflation! Quick, let's cut interest rates to ward off this evil!

–And so it goes. It's a cycle of stupidity that will eventually crush as all.

–How long can this go on, you ask?

–No one knows the answer to that. 10 years is, I think, too optimistic. It all depends on how long central banks can keep the confidence (or the con game) going. But it's a fine line. If, during the next global slowdown, central banks all go for the QE button again, you could see the absurd situation where asset prices go into melt-up mode while at the same time economies go into recession. This would be the result of everyone trying try get out of weakening currencies and buying anything else to preserve their purchasing power.

–The bottom line is that it is crazy. No one has seen anything like this before. Your best bet is to put your biases to one side and expect anything and everything. Because that's what you'll get.

–The next question is on the petrodollar:

'The Petrodollar is used by all at present. There is a new king in Saudi Arabia. What If Russia, Venezuela, and Iran were to dump the petrodollar with the help of the Saudis? What do you think the outcome could be? There has been a lot of comments about this since the US started producing and selling its own oil. China is sitting on the sidelines, just watching.'

–My view on the topic of the petrodollar (which means having oil and energy traded in US dollars on a global basis) is that it's very interesting, but not particularly useful in coming up with an investment strategy. So I don't spend a lot of time thinking about it.

–It's a common topic for many in the blogosphere to hypothesize about the end of the petrodollar, but it's something that never seems to come about, despite the apparent will of oil producing nations to rid themselves of it.

–The petrodollar is a product of the global monetary system that evolved after the Bretton Woods system collapsed in the early 1970s. In 1973, the US promised to protect Saudi Arabia's interests in the Middle East if Saudi Arabia, by far the largest producer of oil at the time, priced its product exclusively in US dollars.

–This reinforced the US dollar's role as the world's reserve currency. It enabled the US to pay for its massive energy needs by issuing US treasuries. This is now an entrenched system. You can't take down the Petrodollar without taking down the whole financial system as we know it.

–The Saudis' relationship with the US has soured in recent years, but it's not like they have an alternative. And they're at loggerheads with Russia and Iran (over Syria) and Iran again (over Yemen), so they are hardly going to cooperate with these two countries. And Venezuela is an economic basket case. They won't be making much noise about the petrodollar anytime soon.

–The US is less dependent on Saudi oil than it used to be but with the oil price at these levels, US production will fall in years to come. That makes the Middle East still very important for the US as an energy importer.

–My guess is that the US knows the danger of being so close to Saudi Arabia. The ruling family is only holding onto power through a generous welfare scheme, one that will hurt its budget a lot more in a low oil price environment. Some estimates suggest the break-even point for the Saudi budget is an oil price of around US$95.

–So you'll probably see more instability in Saudi Arabia in the years to come. This is why the US is in Iraq and starting dialogue with Iran. It wants to diversify the security of its oil supply.

–And yes, China is waiting in the background. China is the largest importer of Saudi Arabian oil. But it's in China's interests to maintain the Petrodollar standard. With a few trillion dollars worth of US treasuries in its back pocket, it's one way for China to pay for its energy needs.

–In short, I can't see it ending anytime soon. When it does, the whole system as you know it will end too.

Courtesy, Greg Canavan, The Daily Reckoning (Australia)

CHAPTER 12.

IGNORANT DEPOSITORS

 I believe silver to be the cheapest, most undervalued asset on the planet. From these current levels I believe any capital in silver is a no brainer. Let's hold off on this thought until next week however, a more pressing thought has come up.

Let's start with a question. Would you ever lend money to someone you knew for a fact was bankrupt? Or, would you lend money to someone who told you to your face they were cooking their own book? Isn't this exactly what you are doing any time you deposit money into most any bank? Without getting long winded on this aspect, you do remember back in 2010 or thereabouts our banks in the U.S. were allowed to outright cook their books? The banks were no longer required to price their portfolios at "marked to market" prices. Since then, they can simply "make up" whatever prices they choose and report those.

It is the same situation in Europe but they have had a little "help" in their fraud. For example let's look at Greek bonds that are held in banks all over Europe. Greece without a doubt cannot mathematically pay back their debt. They do not have enough cash to even make next month's "credit card payment" without an infusion from somewhere. I use this term credit card payment because that is exactly what these are, this week for example is a miniscule 500 million euros, not even half a ham sandwich in the global scheme of things. If they cannot make a payment or they go through a restructuring, or in all probability they cut a deal with the Russians and Chinese followed by "we quit and we aren't paying you" …what are these bonds really worth? Ten cents? Five? Zero?

My point is this, these bonds are carried on balance sheets at 100 cents on the euro!

Banks, including the European Central Bank itself values these bonds at par as if they were pristine a credit. The BIS has allowed sovereign credits within Europe to be carried at par on bank balance sheets. This is clearly bogus. It was my intention to also speak about Spain's short term interest rates just went negative. They were my original thought to "would you lend money to a bankrupt entity?". While writing this, two pieces of news have come out and spotlights my point. Greece has in fact made the April payment, now we wait for the next due date which finance minister Varoufakis says "will be different", what does he mean by "different"? Mr. Tsipras concluded his meeting in Moscow, what exactly was discussed? Greece has also surprised us yesterday by contemplating calling all new debt taken on since 2012 as "odious" . I believe the new amount of debt taken on is over 100 billion euros, does this mean they will just walk away from this post 2012 debt and only service the earlier debt? Was this a part of the discussions in Moscow? Greece will continue to pay on pre 2012 debt but not post debt? Is this debt "justified" being priced at 100% or par or should a minor adjustment be in order?

As you know from previous writings, the Austrian banking system is wobbling because of the rise in the Swiss franc versus the euro. This was caused by Hypo Alpe Adria bank not being able to make a 600 million euro payment. This has affected their counter parties and has since spread. Could this paltry amount take down the Austrian banks?

Do you see what today's exercise is all about? It looks like amounts as small as "millions" which only amount to credit card monthly payments may be enough to torpedo individual banks ...and even a country! The fact that the world is so levered and interconnected means very small "non payments" have the ability to spread and take everything down with it... and it looks like this is exactly what is happening!

I have said all along that our entire financial system was about "collateral" and it would be the realization the collateral was "bad" as the reason for collapse. This is where we are today, extremely small interest payments which cannot be made are about to expose the true value of the underlying "collateral". Just because the regulators have allowed banks to mark their assets to fantasy levels does not mean the bad collateral will not fail. It will. IT ALL WILL! This is the reason "bail in" legislation has been written and put into place all over the world. Because they KNEW when they wrote the legislation they would be forced to use it.

The white knight of "bail outs" will not and can no longer ride in to save ignorant depositors. I use the word "ignorant" because who in their right mind would lend their money at a negative interest rate ...in a debasing currency ...to a bank that lies about their asset quality ...in a system where if one fails they all fail? And on top of this, the regulators, central banks and governments themselves have already written legislation saying "when it comes down, we will take your money to make ourselves whole". Who would do this? I'm pretty sure holding gold is a safer bet but that's just me and everyone knows I wear a tin foil cowboy hat.

CHAPTER 13.

BIT-RESERVE JUST COULD BE THE ANSWER TO OUR "BAIL IN" PROBLEM!

What is Bitreserve?

Bitreserve makes using digital money fast, easy and free.

We're a next-generation financial service. Bitreserve shields you from bitcoin volatility by enabling you to hold bitcoin as the money you use every day. Bitreserve keeps your value safe, while letting you spend your money as bitcoin, and send it to anyone in the world instantly and for free.

With Bitreserve, you can flip back and forth from bitcoin to any of six currencies — gold, dollars, euros, pounds, yen, and yuan. We provide instant, low-cost currency conversions.

Bitcurrencies are as stable as their real-world counterparts, but are connected to the Bitcoin Network. That means you can hold your bitcoin as stable euros or yuan, but still transfer value as bitcoin to bitcoin addresses inside or outside Bitreserve.

Want to buy something for $50? Tip your taxi driver €5? Send a gift of ?4000? Donate £40 to a charity? Settle a bet for one bitcoin? As a Bitreserve Member, you can send and receive bitcurrency for free to and from anyone in the world and make purchases anywhere bitcoin is accepted.

By acting as a bridge between the revolutionary Bitcoin protocol and a full reserve of real-world assets, Bitreserve offers the advantages of digital money with the stability and familiarity of the real-world currency you use every day.

What currencies does Bitreserve support?

With Bitreserve, you can choose to hold bitcoin in a variety of bitcurrencies and bitmetals, yet spend and move your value as bitcoin. See the ful list of available currencies and precious metals below:

Currencies
– U.S. dollars (USD)
– Euros (EUR)
– Pounds (GBP)
– Yuan (CNY)
– Yen (JPY)
– Swiss Franc (CHF)

Precious Metals
– Gold (XAU)
– Silver (XAG)
– Platinum (XPT)
– Palladium (XPL)

Is my bitcoin safe in Bitreserve?

Yes. We take a holistic approach to security at Bitreserve, applying the best practices and technologies to every aspect of our systems, products, installations, networks and people.

For your safety, we don't publish the specifics of our security measures, but our senior management's experience building and running safe and resilient companies is our best defense against bad actors and other risks.

Bitreserve executives have been responsible for the success of dozens of organizations that depend on safeguarding information, money and other stores of value.

Is Bitreserve a bank? What does it mean to maintain a full reserve?

Banks make money by loaning out your deposits for interest. This system is called fractional reserve banking. The obligations a bank has to its depositors do not match the assets the bank holds, since most of those assets are in the form of loans made to generate revenue for the bank. That works fine, as long as everyone pays back their loans and not all depositors withdraw all their money at the same time.

Bitreserve is not a bank. We create digital versions of the money you use every day by maintaining a full reserve of real-world currencies. That means for every dollar, euro, pound, yen, or yuan of bitcurrency in a Member's wallet, Bitreserve holds a real dollar, euro, pound, yen or yuan. Our business model doesn't depend on making loans with the value that enters Bitreserve.

Because we maintain a full reserve of real-world currencies and publish a real-time, verifiable proof of solvency, you can always be sure that your value is safe.

What Members Are Saying

"Love the service. With Bitreserve, we're moving to a better financial system where we can do low cost money transfers."

– Adam G.

"The card system is brilliant and the idea to include all assets in a global account is amazing. This is a truly global wealth management platform, as well as a convenient way to move value around the world."

– Donald M.

A Three Minute Video Explaining How It Works:

https://bitreserve.org/en/how-it-works

*Courtesy, www.**bitreserve.org***

CHAPTER 14.

THE SIX TOO BIG TO FAIL BANKS IN THE U.S. HAVE 278 TRILLION DOLLARS OF EXPOSURE TO DERIVATIVES

THE SIX TOO BIG TO FAIL BANKS IN THE U.S. HAVE 278 TRILLION DOLLARS OF EXPOSURE TO DERIVATIVES

The very same people that caused the last economic crisis have created a 278 **TRILLION** dollar derivatives time bomb that could go off at any moment. When this absolutely colossal bubble does implode, we are going to be faced with the worst economic crash in the history of the United States. During the last financial crisis, our politicians promised us that they would make sure that "too big to fail" would never be a problem again. Instead, as you will see below, those banks have actually gotten far larger since then. So now we **really** can't afford for them to fail. The six banks that I am talking about are JPMorgan Chase, Citibank, Goldman Sachs, Bank of America, Morgan Stanley and Wells Fargo.

When you add up all of their exposure to derivatives, it comes to a grand total of more than 278 trillion dollars. But when you add up all of the assets of all six banks combined, it only comes to a grand total of about 9.8 trillion dollars. In other words, these "too big to fail" banks have exposure to derivatives that is **more than 28 times greater than their total assets**.

This is complete and utter insanity, and yet nobody seems too alarmed about it. For the moment, those banks are still making lots of money and funding the campaigns of our most prominent politicians. Right now there is no incentive for them to stop their incredibly reckless gambling so they are just going to keep on doing it.

So precisely what are "derivatives"? Well, they can be immensely complicated, but I like to simplify things. On a very basic level, a "derivative" is not an investment in anything. When you buy a stock, you are purchasing an ownership interest in a company. When you buy a bond, you are purchasing the debt of a company. But a derivative is quite different. In essence, most derivatives are simply bets about what will or will not happen in the future. The big banks have transformed Wall Street into the biggest casino in the history of the planet, and when things are running smoothly they usually make a whole lot of money.

But there is a fundamental flaw in the system, and I described this in a previous article...

> The big banks use very sophisticated algorithms that are supposed to help them be on the winning side of these bets the vast majority of the time, but these algorithms are not perfect. The reason these algorithms are not perfect is because they are based on assumptions, and those assumptions come from people. They might be really smart people, but they are still just people.

Today, the "too big to fail" banks are being

even more reckless than they were just prior to the financial crash of 2008.

As long as they keep winning, everyone is going to be okay. But when the time comes that their bets start going against them, it is going to be a nightmare for all of us. Our entire economic system is based on the flow of credit, and those banks are at the very heart of that system.

In fact, the five largest banks account for approximately 42 percent of all loans in the United States, and the six largest banks account for approximately 67 percent of all assets in our financial system.

So that is why they are called "too big to fail". We simply cannot afford for them to go out of business.

As I mentioned above, our politicians promised that something would be done about this. But instead, the four largest banks in the country have gotten nearly 40 percent larger since the last time around. The following numbers come from an article in the Los Angeles Times...

> Just before the financial crisis hit, Wells Fargo & Co. had $609 billion in assets. Now it has $1.4 trillion. Bank of America Corp. had $1.7 trillion in assets. That's up to $2.1 trillion.

> And the assets of JPMorgan Chase & Co., the nation's biggest bank, have ballooned to $2.4 trillion from $1.8 trillion.

During this same time period, 1,400 smaller banks have completely disappeared from the banking industry.

So our economic system is now more dependent on the "too big to fail" banks than ever.

To illustrate how reckless the "too big to fail" banks have become, I want to share with you some brand new numbers which come directly from the OCC's most recent quarterly report (see Table 2)...

JPMorgan Chase

Total Assets: $2,573,126,000,000 (about 2.6 trillion dollars)

Total Exposure To Derivatives: $63,600,246,000,000 (**more than 63 trillion dollars**)

Citibank

Total Assets: $1,842,530,000,000 (more than 1.8 trillion dollars)

Total Exposure To Derivatives: $59,951,603,000,000 (**more than 59 trillion dollars**)

Goldman Sachs

Total Assets: $856,301,000,000 (less than a trillion dollars)

Total Exposure To Derivatives: $57,312,558,000,000 (**more than 57 trillion dollars**)

Bank Of America

Total Assets: $2,106,796,000,000 (a little bit more than 2.1 trillion dollars)

Total Exposure To Derivatives: $54,224,084,000,000 (**more than 54 trillion dollars**)

Morgan Stanley

Total Assets: $801,382,000,000 (less than a trillion dollars)

Total Exposure To Derivatives: $38,546,879,000,000 (**more than 38 trillion dollars**)

Wells Fargo

Total Assets: $1,687,155,000,000 (about 1.7 trillion dollars)

Total Exposure To Derivatives: $5,302,422,000,000 (**more than 5 trillion dollars**)

Compared to the rest of them, Wells Fargo looks extremely prudent and rational.

But of course that is not true at all. Wells Fargo is being very reckless, but the others are being so reckless that it makes everyone else pale in comparison.

And these banks are not exactly in good shape for the next financial crisis that is rapidly approaching. The following is an excerpt from a recent Business Insider article…

> The New York Times isn't so sure about the results from the Federal Reserve's latest round of stress tests.
>
> In an editorial published over the weekend, The Times cites data from Thomas Hoenig, vice chairman of the FDIC, who, in contrast to the Federal Reserve, found that **capital ratios at the eight largest banks in the US averaged 4.97% at the end of 2014, far lower than the 12.9% found by the Fed's stress test**.

That doesn't sound good.

So what is up with the discrepancy in the numbers? The New York Times explains…

> The discrepancy is due mainly to differing views of the risk posed by the banks' **vast holdings of derivative contracts** used for hedging and speculation. The Fed, in keeping

with American accounting rules and central bank accords, assumes that gains and losses on **derivatives** generally net out. As a result, most **derivatives** do not show up as assets on banks' balance sheets, an omission that bolsters the ratio of capital to assets.

Mr. Hoenig **uses stricter international accounting rules to value the derivatives**. Those rules do not assume that gains and losses reliably net out. As a result, large **derivative** holdings are shown as assets on the balance sheet, an addition that reduces the ratio of capital to assets to the low levels reported in Mr. Hoenig's analysis.

Derivatives, eh?

Very interesting.

And you know what?

The guys running these big banks can see what is coming.

Just consider the words that JPMorgan Chase chairman and CEO Jamie Dimon wrote to his shareholders not too long ago...

Some things never change — **there will be**

another crisis, and its impact will be felt by the financial market.

The trigger to the next crisis will not be the same as the trigger to the last one – **but there will be another crisis.** Triggering events could be geopolitical (the 1973 Middle East crisis), a recession where the Fed rapidly increases interest rates (the 1980-1982 recession), a commodities price collapse (oil in the late 1980s), the commercial real estate crisis (in the early 1990s), the Asian crisis (in 1997), so-called "bubbles" (the 2000 Internet bubble and the 2008 mortgage/housing bubble), etc. While the past crises had different roots (you could spend a lot of time arguing the degree to which geopolitical, economic or purely financial factors caused each crisis), they generally had a strong effect across the financial markets

In the same letter, Dimon mentioned "derivatives moved by enormous players and rapid computerized trades" as part of the reason why our system is so vulnerable to another crisis.

If this is what he truly believes, why is his firm being so incredibly reckless?

Perhaps someone should ask him that.

Interestingly, Dimon also discussed the possibility of a Greek exit from the eurozone...

> "We must be prepared for a potential exit," J. P. Morgan Chief Executive Officer Jamie Dimon said. in his annual letter to shareholders. "We continually stress test our company for possible repercussions resulting from such an event."

This is something that I have been warning about for a long time.

And of course Dimon is not the only prominent banker warning of big problems ahead. German banking giant Deutsche Bank is also sounding the alarm...

> With a U.S. profit recession expected in the first half of 2015 and investors unlikely to pay up for stocks, the risk of a stock market drop of 5% to 10% is rising, Deutsche Bank says.

> That's the warning Deutsche Bank market strategist David Bianco zapped out to clients today before the opening bell on Wall Street.

Bianco expects earnings for the broad Standard & Poor's 500-stock index to contract in the first half of 2015 — the first time that's happened since 2009 during the financial crisis. And the combination of soft earnings and his belief that investors won't pay top dollar for stocks in a market that is already trading at above-average valuations is a recipe for a short-term pullback on Wall Street.

The truth is that we are in the midst of a historic stock market bubble, and we are witnessing all sorts of patterns in the financial markets which also emerged back in 2008 right before the financial crash in the fall of that year.

When some of the most prominent bankers at some of the biggest banks on the entire planet start issuing ominous warnings, that is a clear sign that time is running out. The period of relative stability that we have been enjoying has been fun, and hopefully it will last just a little while longer. But at some point it will end, and then the pain will begin.

Courtesy, Michael Snyder

CHAPTER 15.

TIME IS RUNNING OUT AS THE ECB PREPARES TO STEAL GREEK BANK DEPOSITS

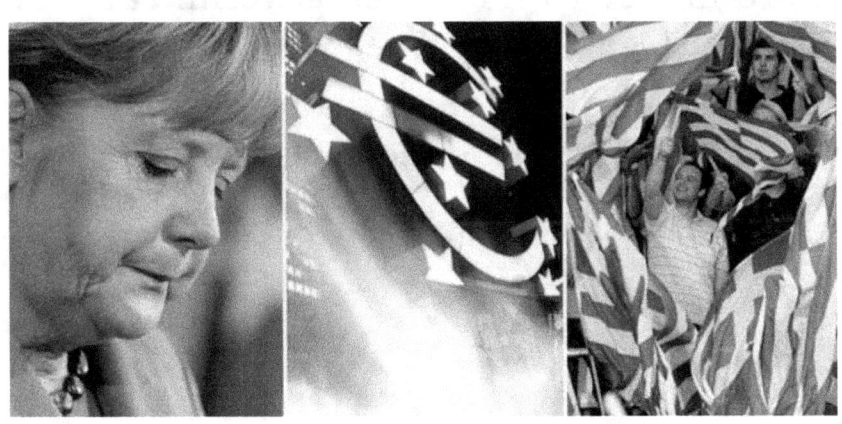

Today the man who <u>first predicted Greek bank deposits would be stolen</u> just issued a warning about the crisis in Greece that is threatening the global financial system. He also warns that time is has just about run out to solve the crisis.

James Turk: "Everybody is playing hardball in Greece, Eric. The standoff between the Greek government and its creditors has reached crisis levels. All we can do now is wait to see who will blink first. The Greek government has acknowledged that it has nearly run out of money….

"Greece is unable to borrow more money from the ECB or from Greek banks, which have been instructed by the ECB not to lend more money to the Greek government. The money the Greek government is receiving from taxes is its sole source of cash, and these tax receipts are below what the Greek government has been expecting.

The Troika Is The Problem

On the other side of the stand-off is the so-called "troika" of the EU, ECB and IMF, which refuses to give ground. They are requiring Greece to stick with the terms negotiated by previous Greek governments and repay its debts on schedule. But the only way those debts can be repaid is if the troika loans the next €7.5 billion tranche under its rescue program.

All the troika is doing is piling more debt upon the debt mountain that has already forced Greece to its knees. By giving Greece more loans to repay previous debts, the troika hopes that it can make Greece appear solvent, when it is not. The bottom line is that Greece does not have the financial capacity to repay its debts.

ECB Still Preparing To Snatch Greek Bank Deposits

The ECB has not yet taken the nuclear option by forcing a bail-in of depositor money in Greek banks to repay the ECB's loans to Greece, but that moment remains close. It is the only way that the ECB will get its money back.

Importantly, ECB president Mario Draghi has confirmed that the ECB's exposure to Greece is €110 billion, which is one side of the all-important equation that will determine when the Greek banks get nationalized. The other side of the equation is the current level of deposits in Greek banks.

Time Is Running Out As The ECB Prepares To Steal Greek Bank Deposits

There have not been any recent reports as

to what remains on deposit in the Greek banking system. The best guess seems to be that total deposits are about €130 billion, but deposits continue to shrink. So even though the ECB is not making more loans, these two totals are still converging. They will not be allowed to cross. The ECB will take depositor money before these two lines cross to repay its loans to Greece.

Greece Is The Biggest Risk To The Global Economy

It is clear that Greece is teetering on the brink of default. Its bonds have been downgraded again and are now deep into junk status territory. And despite the EU saying Greek banks are solvent, every indication is that much of the Greek banking system is largely insolvent and beyond hope as the crumbling Greek economy puts more bank loans in jeopardy.

A few weeks ago the British Chancellor, George Osborne, told Yanis Varoufakis, the Greek Finance Minister, that Greece is becoming the biggest risk to the global economy. And the risk now is even worse as Greece runs out of money and prepares for a default on its €325 billion of debt, which looks not only inevitable, but imminent."

Courtesy, Eric King, KingWorldNews.com

CHAPTER 16.

JOHN WILLIAMS UPDATES HIS VIEWS ON DEFLATION, HYPERINFLATION AND THE FALL OF THE U.S. DOLLAR

---

http://news.goldseek.com/radio/
1428897600.php

Listen to John Williams on Gold Seek Radio, link above.

Summary:

- John Williams guests on Goldseek.com Radio with dire thoughts on the veracity of the official economic figures.

- The domestic economy has not recovered

– virtually every economic indicator remains stagnant since 2009.

- According to the Wall Street Journal, the typical American household spends 62% merely to pay housing / grocery bills, an unsustainable burden

- While corporations have recovered from the recession, the everyday consumer has not.

- Without real income growth the largest component of the domestic economy, consumption (over 70%) could falter.

- The US Dollar will likely reverse course, which will result with runaway inflation and hyperinflation.

- The best defense is a good offense – only gold and silver investments can protect investors from the sea change event.

- His 2015 economic forecast includes a sharp decrease in economic growth / output, causing Fed officials to further delay rate hikes.

Leading   alternative   economist   from

ShadowStats.com, doubts the veracity of the official economic figures, noting that the domestic economy has not recovered as our officials contend. On the contrary, his analysis shows that virtually every economic indicator remains stagnant since 2009. He adds support to his thesis, via moribund consumer income levels, given the soaring cost of basic necessities.

According to the Wall Street Journal, the typical American household spends 62% merely to pay housing / grocery bills, an unsustainable burden – reminiscent of serfs-like burdens in the feudal system. Therefore, while corporations have recovered from the recession, the everyday consumer has not. Without real income growth the largest component of the domestic economy, consumption (over 70%) could falter. The startlingly vertical ascent of the US Dollar will likely reverse course , in turn increasing inflation to the benefit of gold, silver, crude oil and commodities investors.

His work indicates that a dollar collapse is imminent, which will result with runaway inflation and hyperinflation – only gold and silver investments can protect investors from the sea change event. His 2015 economic forecast includes a sharp decrease in economic growth / output, causing Fed officials to further delay rate hikes.

Courtesy, Goldseek.com

CHAPTER 17.

UNSOUND BANKING: WHY MOST OF THE WORLD'S BANKS ARE HEADED FOR COLLAPSE

You're likely thinking that a discussion of "sound banking" will be a bit boring. Well, banking should be boring. And we're sure officials at central banks all over the world today—many of whom have trouble sleeping—wish it were.

This brief article will explain why the world's banking system is unsound, and what differentiates a sound from an unsound bank. I suspect not one person in 1,000 actually understands the difference. As a result, the world's economy is now based upon unsound banks dealing in unsound currencies. Both have degenerated considerably from their origins.

Modern banking emerged from the goldsmithing trade of the Middle Ages. Being a goldsmith required a working inventory of precious metal, and managing that inventory profitably required expertise in buying and selling metal and storing it securely. Those capacities segued easily into the business of lending and borrowing gold, which is to say the business of lending and borrowing money.

Most people today are only dimly aware that until the early 1930s, gold coins were used in everyday commerce by the general public. In addition, gold backed most national currencies at a fixed rate of convertibility. Banks were just another business—nothing special. They were distinguished from other enterprises only by the fact they stored, lent, and borrowed gold coins, not as a sideline but as a primary business. Bankers had become goldsmiths without the hammers.

Bank deposits, until quite recently, fell strictly into two classes, depending on the preference of the depositor and the terms offered by banks: time deposits, and demand deposits. Although the distinction between them has been lost in recent years, respecting the difference is a critical element of sound banking practice.

Time Deposits. With a time deposit—a savings account, in essence—a customer contracts to leave his money with the banker for a specified period. In return, he receives a specified fee (interest) for his risk, for his inconvenience, and as consideration for allowing the banker the use of the depositor's money. The banker, secure in knowing he has a specific amount of gold for a specific amount of time, is able to lend it; he'll do so at an interest rate high enough to cover expenses (including the interest promised to the depositor), fund a loan-loss reserve, and if all goes according to plan, make a profit.

A time deposit entails a commitment by both parties. The depositor is locked in until the due date. How could a sound banker promise to give a time depositor his money back on demand and without penalty when he's planning to lend it out?

In the business of accepting time deposits, a banker is a dealer in credit, acting as an intermediary between lenders and borrowers. To avoid loss, bankers customarily preferred to lend on productive assets, whose earnings offered assurance that the borrower could cover the interest as it came due. And they were willing to lend only a fraction of the value of a pledged asset, to ensure a margin of safety for the principal. And only for a limited time—such as against the harvest of a crop or the sale of an inventory. And finally, only to people of known good character—the first line of defense against fraud. Long-term loans were the province of bond syndicators.

That's time deposits. Demand deposits were a completely different matter.

Demand Deposits. Demand deposits were so called because, unlike time deposits, they were payable to the customer on demand. These are the basis of checking accounts. The banker doesn't pay interest on the money, because he supposedly never has the use of it; to the contrary, he necessarily charged the depositor a fee for:

1. Assuming the responsibility of keeping the money safe, available for immediate withdrawal, and

1. Administering the transfer of the money if the depositor so chooses by either writing a check or passing along a warehouse receipt that represents the gold on deposit.

An honest banker should no more lend out demand deposit money than Allied Van and Storage should lend out the furniture you've paid it to store. The warehouse receipts for gold were called *banknotes*. When a government issued them, they were called *currency*. Gold bullion, gold coinage, banknotes, and currency together constituted the society's supply of transaction *media*. But its amount was strictly limited by the amount of gold actually available to people.

Sound principles of banking are identical to sound principles of warehousing any kind of merchandise, whether it's autos, potatoes, or books. Or money. There's nothing mysterious about sound banking. But banking all over the world has been fundamentally *un*sound since government-sponsored central banks came to dominate the financial system.

Central banks are a linchpin of today's world financial system. By purchasing government debt, banks can allow the state—for a while—to finance its activities without taxation. On the surface, this appears to be a "free lunch." But it's actually quite pernicious and is the engine of currency debasement.

Central banks may seem like a permanent

part of the cosmic landscape, but in fact they are a recent invention. The US Federal Reserve, for instance, didn't exist before 1913.

UNSOUND BANKING

Fraud can creep into any business. A banker, seeing other people's gold sitting idle in his vault, might think, "What is the point of taking gold out of the ground from a mine, only to put it back into the ground in a vault?" People are writing checks against it and using his banknotes. But the gold itself seldom moves. A restless banker might conclude that, even though it might be a fraud on depositors (depending on exactly what the bank has promised them), he could easily create lots more banknotes and lend them out, and keep 100% of the interest for himself.

Left solely to their own devices, some bankers would try that. But most would be careful not to go too far, since the game would end abruptly if any doubt emerged about the bank's ability to hand over gold on demand. The arrival of central banks eased that fear by introducing a lender of last resort. Because the central bank is always standing by with credit, bankers are free to make promises they know they might not be able to keep on their own.

HOW BANKING WORKS TODAY

In the past, when a bank created too much currency out of nothing, people eventually would notice, and a "bank run" would materialize. But when a central bank authorizes all banks to do the same thing, that's less likely—unless it becomes known that an individual bank has made some really foolish loans.

Central banks were originally justified—especially the creation of the Federal Reserve in the US—as a device for economic stability. The occasional chastisement of imprudent bankers and their foolish customers was an excuse to get government into the banking business. As has happened in so many cases, an occasional and local problem was "solved" by making it systemic and housing it in a national institution. It's loosely analogous to the way the government handles the problem of forest fires: extinguishing them quickly provides an immediate and visible benefit. But the delayed and forgotten consequence of doing so is that it allows decades of deadwood to accumulate. Now when a fire starts, it can be a once-in-a-century conflagration.

Banking all over the world now operates on a "fractional reserve" system. In our earlier example, our sound banker kept a 100% reserve against demand deposits: he held one ounce of gold in his vault for every one-ounce banknote he issued. And he could only lend the proceeds of time deposits, not demand deposits. A "fractional reserve" system can't work in a free market; it has to be legislated. And it can't work where banknotes are redeemable in a commodity, such as gold; the banknotes have to be "legal tender" or strictly paper money that can be created by fiat.

The fractional reserve system is why banking is more profitable than normal businesses. In any industry, rich average returns attract competition, which reduces returns. A banker can lend out a dollar, which a businessman might use to buy a widget. When that seller of the widget re-deposits the dollar, a banker can lend it out at interest again. The good news for the banker is that his earnings are compounded several times over. The bad news is that, because of the pyramided leverage, a default can cascade. In each country, the central bank periodically changes the percentage reserve (theoretically, from 100% down to 0% of deposits) that banks must keep with it, according to how the bureaucrats in charge perceive the state of the economy.

In any event, in the US (and actually most everywhere in the world), protection against runs on banks isn't provided by sound practices, but by laws. In 1934, to restore confidence in commercial banks, the US government instituted the Federal Deposit Insurance Corporation (FDIC) deposit insurance in the amount of $2,500 per depositor per bank, eventually raising coverage to today's $250,000. In Europe, €100,000 is the amount guaranteed by the state.

FDIC insurance covers about $9.3 trillion of deposits, but the institution has assets of only $25 billion. That's less than one cent on the dollar. I'll be surprised if the FDIC doesn't go bust and need to be recapitalized by the government. That money—many billions—will likely be created out of thin air by selling Treasury debt to the Fed.

The fractional reserve banking system, with all of its unfortunate attributes, is critical to the world's financial system as it is currently structured. You can plan your life around the fact the world's governments and central banks will do everything they can to maintain confidence in the financial system. To do so, they must prevent a deflation at all costs. And to do that, they will continue printing up more dollars, pounds, euros, yen, and what-have-you.

Editor's Note: While currency crises, bank runs and episodes of economic collapse are devastating to paper assets, they often hand us opportunities to pick up hard assets on the very cheap.

Each month we scour the world looking for the best crisis-born opportunities from fundamentally sound businesses whose stock prices have been hammered down by fear, crisis, and politically caused distortions.

Founded on the principles that made a Doug Casey a bold fortune, *Crisis Speculator* delivers boots-on-the-ground reporting and opportunities from Albania to Zambia.

Courtesy, Doug Casey

CHAPTER 18.

THE TRANS-PACIFIC PARTNERSHIP AND THE DEATH OF THE REPUBLIC

The United States shall guarantee to every State in this Union a Republican Form of Government. — Article IV, Section 4, US Constitution

A republican form of government is one in which power resides in elected officials representing the citizens, and government leaders exercise power according to the rule of law. In *The Federalist Papers*, James Madison defined a republic as "a government which derives all its powers directly or indirectly from the great body of the people . . . ."

On April 22, 2015, the Senate Finance Committee approved a bill to fast-track the Trans-Pacific Partnership (TPP), a massive trade agreement that would override our republican form of government and hand judicial and legislative authority to a foreign three-person panel of corporate lawyers.

The secretive TPP is an agreement with Mexico, Canada, Japan, Singapore and seven other countries that affects 40% of global markets. Fast-track authority could now go to the full Senate for a vote as early as next week. Fast-track means Congress will be prohibited from amending the trade deal, which will be put to a simple up or down majority vote. Negotiating the TPP in secret and fast-tracking it through Congress is considered necessary to secure its passage, since if the public had time to review its onerous provisions, opposition would mount and defeat it.

Abdicating the Judicial Function to Corporate Lawyers

James Madison wrote in *The Federalist Papers*:

The accumulation of all powers, legislative, executive, and judiciary, in the same hands, . . . may justly be pronounced the very definition of tyranny. . . . "Were the power of judging joined with the legislative, the life and liberty of the subject would be exposed to arbitrary control, for *the judge* would then be *the legislator*. . . ."

And that, from what we now know of the TPP's secret provisions, will be its dire effect.

The most controversial provision of the TPP is the Investor-State Dispute Settlement (ISDS) section, which strengthens existing ISDS procedures. ISDS first appeared in a bilateral trade agreement in 1959. According to *The Economist*, ISDS gives foreign firms a special right to apply to a secretive tribunal of highly paid corporate lawyers for compensation whenever the government passes a law to do things that hurt corporate profits — such things as discouraging smoking, protecting the environment or preventing a nuclear catastrophe.

Arbitrators are paid $600-700 an hour, giving them little incentive to dismiss cases; and the secretive nature of the arbitration process and the lack of any requirement to consider precedent gives wide scope for creative judgments.

To date, the highest ISDS award has been for $2.3 billion to Occidental Oil Company against the government of Ecuador over its termination of an oil-concession contract, this although the termination was apparently legal. Still in arbitration is a demand by Vattenfall, a Swedish utility that operates two nuclear plants in Germany, for compensation of €3.7 billion ($4.7 billion) under the ISDS clause of a treaty on energy investments, after the German government decided to shut down its nuclear power industry following the Fukushima disaster in Japan in 2011.

Under the TPP, however, even larger judgments can be anticipated, since the sort of "investment" it protects includes not just "the commitment of capital or other resources" but "the expectation of gain or profit." That means the rights of corporations in other countries extend not just to their factories and other "capital" but to the profits they expect to receive there.

In an article posted by Yves Smith, Joe Firestone poses some interesting hypotheticals:

Under the TPP, could the US government be sued and be held liable if it decided to stop issuing Treasury debt and financed deficit spending in some other way (perhaps by quantitative easing or by issuing trillion dollar coins)? Why not, since some private companies would lose profits as a result?

Under the TPP or the TTIP (the Transatlantic Trade and Investment Partnership under negotiation with the European Union), would the Federal Reserve be sued if it failed to bail out banks that were too big to fail?

Firestone notes that under the Netherlands-Czech trade agreement, the Czech Republic was sued in an investor-state dispute for failing to bail out an insolvent bank in which the complainant had an interest. The investor company was awarded $236 million in the dispute settlement. What might the damages be, asks Firestone, if the Fed decided to let the Bank of America fail, and a Saudi-based investment company decided to sue?

Abdicating the Legislative Function to Multinational Corporations

Just the threat of this sort of massive damage award could be enough to block prospective legislation. But the TPP goes further and takes on the legislative function directly, by forbidding specific forms of regulation.

Public Citizen observes that the TPP would provide big banks with a backdoor means of watering down efforts to re-regulate Wall Street, after deregulation triggered the worst financial crisis since the Great Depression:

> The TPP would forbid countries from banning particularly risky financial products, such as the toxic derivatives that led to the $183 billion government bailout of AIG. It would prohibit policies to prevent banks from becoming "too big to fail," and threaten the use of "firewalls" to prevent banks that keep

our savings accounts from taking hedge-fund-style bets.

The TPP would also restrict capital controls, an essential policy tool to counter destabilizing flows of speculative money. . . . And the deal would prohibit taxes on Wall Street speculation, such as the proposed Robin Hood Tax that would generate billions of dollars' worth of revenue for social, health, or environmental causes.

Clauses on dispute settlement in earlier free trade agreements have been invoked to challenge efforts to regulate big business. The fossil fuel industry is seeking to overturn Quebec's ban on the ecologically destructive practice of fracking. Veolia, the French behemoth known for building a tram network to serve Israeli settlements in occupied East Jerusalem, is contesting increases in Egypt's minimum wage. The tobacco maker Philip Morris is suing against anti-smoking initiatives in Uruguay and Australia.

The TPP would empower not just foreign manufacturers but foreign financial firms to attack financial policies in foreign tribunals, demanding taxpayer compensation for regulations that they claim frustrate their expectations and inhibit their profits.

Preempting Government Sovereignty

What is the justification for this encroachment on the sovereign rights of government? Allegedly, ISDS is necessary in order to increase foreign investment. But as noted in *The Economist*, investors can protect themselves by purchasing political-risk insurance. Moreover, Brazil continues to receive sizable foreign investment despite its long-standing refusal to sign any treaty with an ISDS mechanism. Other countries are beginning to follow Brazil's lead.

In an April 22nd report from the Center for Economic and Policy Research, gains from multilateral trade liberalization were shown to be very small, equal to only about 0.014% of consumption, or about $.43 per person per month. And that assumes that any benefits are distributed uniformly across the economic spectrum. In fact, transnational corporations get the bulk of the benefits, at the expense of most of the world's population.

Something else besides attracting investment money and encouraging foreign trade seems to be going on. The TPP would destroy our republican form of government under the rule of law, by elevating the rights of investors – also called the rights of "capital" – above the rights of the citizens.

That means that TPP is blatantly unconstitutional. But as Joe Firestone observes, neo-liberalism and corporate contributions seem to have blinded the deal's proponents so much that they cannot see they are selling out the sovereignty of the United States to foreign and multinational corporations.

Courtesy, Ellen Brown

CHAPTER 19.

WHAT WILL HAPPEN TO YOU WHEN THE DOLLAR COLLAPSES?

Historically, when a nation's debt exceeds its ability to repay even the interest, it can be assumed that the currency will collapse. Typically, governments exacerbate the situation by printing large amounts of currency notes in an effort to inflate the problem away, or at least postpone it.

The greater the level of debt, the more dramatic the inflation must be to counter it. The more dramatic the inflation, the greater the danger that hyperinflation will take place. No government has ever been able to control hyperinflation. If it occurs, it does so quickly and *always* ends with a crash.

Although there are observers (myself included) who frequently discuss what a reserve-currency crash would mean to the world, there is little or no discussion as to how this would impact people on the street level, and perhaps that discussion should begin.

When currencies crash, the state often tries to float a new currency. Sometimes, it's accepted, sometimes not. Generally, the people of the country (and those trading within the country) move immediately to "the next best thing." In 2009, when the Zimbabwe dollar crashed, several currencies were used, but the US dollar was the clear favourite, as it was the world's reserve currency and therefore the most "spendable" currency.

Not surprisingly, the Zimbabwean government fought the use of the dollar, as they wanted to retain control of the economy and the people. People were therefore penalised for using the US dollar and other currencies.

And that's what most governments do, but

here's where that idea usually falls down: First, the "black-market" currency is so desired by the now-jaded citizens that they do all they can to avoid the *new* official currency. Soon, most transactions, although illegal, are undertaken in the black-market currency. Second, since no one really wants the new currency, even the political leaders are soon using the black-market currency.

Ultimately, the black-market currency is legalised (since it's the only truly workable solution), and it often becomes the unofficial currency, if not actually the official one.

FIRST, THE EURO CRASH

It's safe to say that the EU, the US, and quite a few other jurisdictions are nearing currency crashes, and in all likelihood, the euro will go before the dollar. So, unless the EU has already prearranged a new euro, the US dollar might well be chosen as an immediate solution to the problem, as the US dollar is presently recognised and traded throughout Europe. Therefore, a relatively painless transfer could be made.

THEN, THE DOLLAR CRASH

However, the dollar, which is presently praised as being a sound currency, is really only sound in relation to the euro (and some other lesser currencies). Once its less stable brother, the euro, collapses, the dollar will be exposed.

As the US dollar is a fiat currency and is on the ropes, the US (and any other country that is using the dollar as its primary currency when the time comes) will experience a currency emergency *at the street level* that will be unprecedented.

- The big question that is generally not being discussed is: The day after the crash (and thereafter), what will be the currency that is used to buy a bag of groceries, a tank of petrol, a meal at a restaurant? Certainly, the *need* will be immediate and will be on a national level in each impacted country, affecting everyone.

AND THEN...

I have discussed for some time that the US

will be prepared ahead of time with a new, electronic currency. This will serve three purposes:

- It will allow the US government to create a currency system that disallows the holding of tradable currency by the population—that is, a debit card would be created by banks through which *all* transactions must pass, assuring that *all* transactions are processed by (and thereby subject to the control of) a bank.

- It will allow the US government to blame paper currencies for the crash, in order to distract the public from recognising that the government itself is the culprit.

- It will allow the US government to have knowledge of every penny earned and spent by any individual or organization, allowing for direct-debit income taxation.

If the US does institute such a system, US citizens will then become the most economically controlled people in the world, overnight.

It's likely that a black-market system would spontaneously be created by US citizens in order to bypass the new government system. A portion of daily trade would occur under the table. It would unquestionably be made illegal, and we can only speculate as to how prevalent it would become: 10% of all transactions? 30%? Anyone's guess. Certainly, the government would crack down, and penalties might become severe.

Elsewhere in the world, there would be greater freedom, but what would their currencies be? There are many countries that presently use the US dollar as one of their official currencies. After a crash, the greater the link to the US dollar, the greater the loss of economic freedom, although, in most such countries, the government is likely to be less efficient than in the US, which would work in favour of the individual.

Such countries would also have the option of switching from the dollar to another dominant currency. With the euro and dollar gone, that currency might be the Chinese yuan. The difficulty with this possibility is that, presently, the yuan is not in common use on the street.

Adoption of a currency such as the yuan would require a sudden switch in monetary policy, complete with teething problems. However, recent developments amongst the BRICS and others indicate that many countries are already seeing the writing on the wall and are readying themselves for the use of the yuan as an alternate.

A RETURN TO PRECIOUS METALS AS CURRENCY?

A further possibility is taking place in **Mexico** today. Mexico is remonetising silver. A one-ounce pure silver Libertad coin will function in parallel to (and be interchangeable with) the existing paper peso. Banks will value the Libertad daily, based upon the silver price. Thus, Mexico will create a legal way for its citizens to protect themselves against devaluation of the peso, whilst creating an internal protection against currency crashes in other countries.

If the Mexican government remains

consistent in its plan, it will do more than simply help stabilize Mexico economically; it will serve as an example to other countries that when the Goliaths of the euro and US dollar fall, there is a *very* sound alternative.

Further, the more countries that follow this policy, the more silver (and for that matter, gold) would become an international currency. It would matter little to a petrol station owner in **Canada**, **Australia**, or **Chile** whether his till was filled with coins marked, "Mexico," or whether they said "**Iceland**," "**New Zealand**," or "**South Africa**." After all, an ounce of silver is an ounce of silver, no matter what the issuing country is.

As the Great Unravelling proceeds, we would be wise to monitor what happens with the Libertad in Mexico and watch for a similar return to precious metals in other jurisdictions. As this development progresses, we might wish to consider that, whatever jurisdictions are the most forceful in demanding the continued use of doomed paper currencies (or, worse, transferring into electronic currencies), we may choose to store our wealth, no matter how great or small, in a safer jurisdiction. Further, we may choose to reside in a jurisdiction where a currency crisis will be less likely to occur; to live under a government that does not seek to monitor and tax our every economic transaction.

Editor's note: To help you protect your life savings from a drop in the dollar, and depending on one currency and the whims of one government, we've prepared a free, in-depth video presentation called, "Internationalizing Your Assets."

You'll discover how easy, and essential, it is to move a portion of your savings overseas and protect yourself from rising taxes, capital controls, asset forfeiture, and even predatory lawsuits. Doug Casey and Peter Schiff round out our all-star panel of experts.

Courtesy, Jeff Thomas, International Man

CHAPTER 20.

BANKS PLAY THE MUSIC IN THE ECONOMIC GAME OF MUSICAL CHAIRS

–It sure puts the debate about how much capital Australian banks should hold in an interesting light. Here's the recent news: The banks are coming under pressure to raise capital (money) to offset against their loan books.

–This is the view of those who think higher capital ratios will put the banks in a stronger position if a big downturn hits the economy. *The Australian Financial Review* reported this morning that:

'*Banks should do their bit and raise equity to lower*

the risks to the economy posed by a toppy property market and overextended households, the local head of giant bond manager PIMCO says.

'The opinion comes as UBS analysts warn that continued strength in property prices would increase the banking sector's vulnerability to an economic shock and strengthen the case for further regulatory intervention.'

–Sounds comforting to read. But don't believe it. Even if the banks do raise the money, it won't prevent the cyclical boom bust nature of the economy.

–You don't have to believe me. I have a book on my desk, *Where Does Money Come From?*, co-authored by banking expert Richard Werner. It has a whole chapter on why capital adequacies don't work.

–We'll get to why that is in a sec. First we need to make a quick tour to get the historical irony of all this. The requirement for banks to hold a certain level of capital came about in the 1980s under the original 'Basel Accords'.

–A bank holds capital to cover loans that go into default. But an individual bank can put an indirect limit on the amount of loans it can make (read: credit it can create).

–When they hit this constraint, did the bankers sit around wondering what to do? Did they whistle Dixie as the loans they had already made slowly matured?

–Er…no. They found a way to bend the rules. Thus came the 'securitisation' of mortgage loans that led to the subprime crisis of 2007. You remember, the one that collapsed the banking system around the world.

–By selling on the loans to investors, the banks were able to get them off their books, meet their capital requirement and therefore make new loans. Profits, and share prices, went up accordingly.

–Underneath the shiny veneer, the system was rotting at the core. One reason is that it divorced the traditional long term relationship between the lender (the bank) from the borrower. That's why the big banks became so reckless in who they lent money to.

–They no longer bore the credit risk. That distinction belonged to the suckers like pension funds who actually believed the garbage loans the banks made were 'Triple A'.

–Now let's come back to today. According to the Basel rules, every time a bank makes a loan it has to set aside a certain amount of capital. This money can come from retained profits or money raised from investors (equity).

–A profitable bank can use its retained earnings to hold more capital, which means it can lend more, which means more profit and then higher capital again.

–Not only that, the amount of capital a bank holds depends on the type of loan. A bank has to set aside more capital against a business loan than it does against a property loan.

–That's because the bank can obviously seize the property if the loan goes bad. The future income stream from a business is less uncertain in terms of value. So property loans are lower 'risk-weighted' and far more valuable to the bank.

— Be aware there is also a level of 'self-assessment' in this process. Banks can finesse how much capital they need to set aside according to their own risk models. Obviously, they have an incentive to choose the lower option. Are regulators surprised investor loans to real estate are booming?

–But the point of today's *Daily Reckoning* is to explore why higher capital ratios won't work. The heart of it is that it doesn't limit credit creation.

–This is how the writers put it in *Where Does Money Come From?*:

'If regulators in the future impose higher capital adequacy requirements as a counter-cyclical "macro-prudential" policy, banks will find it easier to raise more capital, as the money to purchase newly issued preferred shares, for instance, is ultimately created by the banking system, and an

increasing amount is created during boom times (hence the boom in the first place).'

–In other words, regulators aren't hitting the banks where they hurt. The only real meaningful reform is to take away the banks' power to create credit, or change the incentives to where they allocate credit in the economy.

–That is to say, the property Ponzi scheme we're slowly building down here in Australia is still running full steam ahead. Early investors will make a killing, but it's a game of musical chairs in the end.

Courtesy, Callum Newman, The Daily Reckoning Australia

CHAPTER 21.

THE END OF CASH?

Money velocity in its simplest terms is a measurement of how fast money is moving through the economy. Another way of looking it is that money velocity is simply a comparison between GDP and money supply. If money velocity is falling then that tells us money supply is increasing at a faster rate than GDP.

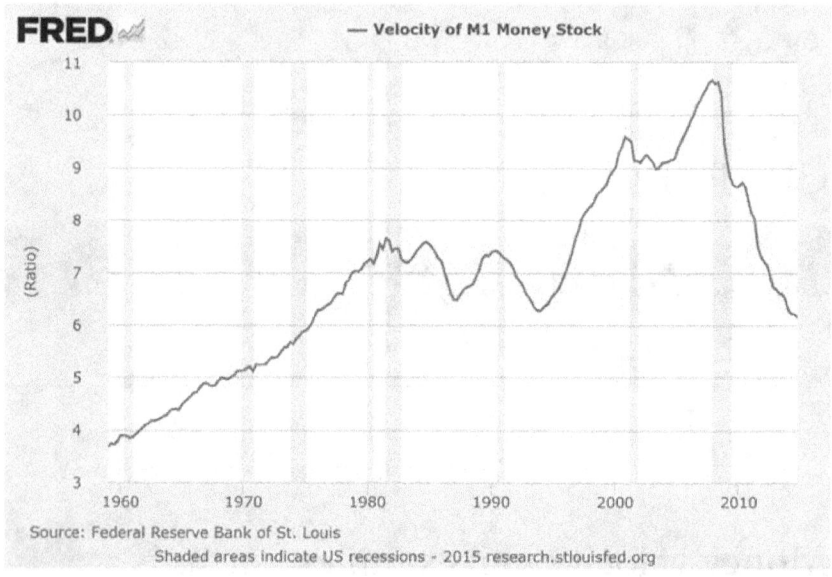

Source: www.stlouisfed.org

M1 is notes and coins in circulation, plus traveler's cheques, demand deposits and other chequable accounts. A rising velocity is a sign that the economy is relatively healthy whereas a falling velocity might be an indication of a slowing economy or an underperforming economy.

The velocity of M1 is back down at levels seen during the 1980's and early 1990's recessions. The reality is that it may even be worse. The chart below shows the velocity of money over the past century. This chart uses M2, which is M1 plus savings accounts, time deposits less than $100,000 and money market accounts for individuals. The picture it shows could be of concern as it shows that the velocity of money has fallen below the levels of the 1950's and 1960's and is trending into the territory of the Great Depression and War of the 1930's and 1940's. Note as well how the velocity of M2 was trending negatively during the roaring twenties. Could it have been a harbinger of things to come?

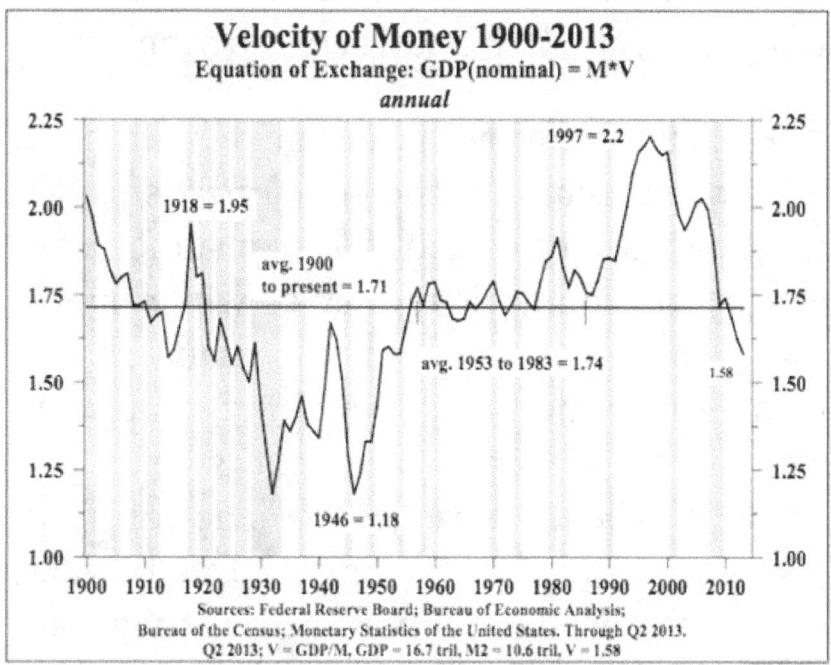

Source: www.bea.gov , www.stlouisfed.org

A falling velocity of money is not just limited

to the US. In the Euro zone and Japan and even China and Canada money velocity has been falling. All of this comes against a backdrop of some of the biggest stimulus ever known. The US has gone through QE1, 2 and 3. Japan it seems has been on QE for years. The Euro zone and China have had their own versions of QE. Some have called the QE's a tsunami of money. And global debt has grown by $57 trillion since the financial collapse of 2008. Yet the western economies remain moribund, stuck in neutral or slowing again.

The illusion of growth can only be purchased with more debt. Yet the consumer is for the most part buried in debt. The consumer is not exactly hoarding his money as while savings rates have improved they remain sharply below earlier periods. If anything as numbers show in the US, mortgage debt is being paid off (or maybe just written off). The consumer just seems to be trying to tread water. Corporations are hoarding money and governments in Europe and elsewhere have been preaching austerity. If the western economies were healthy, the velocity of money would be growing. There is a limit it seems to credit growth, yet what growth there has been has been insufficient.

Despite all the debt that has been created since the financial crisis of 2008 it seems it is not enough or the economies would have expanded further. When the world finally came out of the Great Depression and War it was a big increase in production and people being put to work in good jobs that grew the economies of the 1950's and 1960's. Then came the inflationary 1970's and to get their way out of the mess debt began to expand. That worked during the 1980's and also into the 1990's but it all began to falter badly following the high tech/internet collapse of 2000-2002. Another massive debt binge helped create the housing bubble that took us to the financial crash of 2008. And now this time despite massive injections of QE and debt growth the western economies are at best moribund with low growth.

It is against this backdrop that I read that there is according to some "a relentless war against cash payments". By all accounts, it is accelerating and there are those who would like to eliminate the use of cash all together. If the velocity of money is falling with cash still circulating who knows what it would to do to a cashless society. Tech "geeks" might love a cashless society but for many it is their means of survival and it would most likely be the end of privacy, as we know it.

Ostensibly, the reason for ending cash is to put a stop to terrorists, jihadists, drug dealers, money launderers, tax evaders and many others. But the reality of it would be that everyone would be forced to make their payments through the financial system and allow governments to track their citizens. Many would most likely not object to it. But it would most likely impact everyone including many in a negative way.

It is difficult to say where the call for a cashless society came as it is an idea that has been around for some time. But the cry has come loud from the Euro zone where interest rates are now negative. When interest rates are below zero it costs money to keep your funds in the bank. Cash already pays nothing so holding cash is preferred to keeping your money in a financial institution that charges you. Out of this, Citibank's Willem Buiter has suggested that a) abolish currency, b) tax currency, and c) remove the fixed exchange rate between currency and central bank reserves/deposits.

It is not surprising to learn then that some pension funds and others in the Euro zone want to withdraw their money from the bank and hold it in cash as they realized it is cheaper to store and move cash then it is to pay the bank the negative interest rates. There are numerous stories and blogs around the internet that highlight what is becoming known as "the war on cash."

- France's finance minister Michel Sapin blamed the Charlie Hebdo murders on the attacker's ability to buy weapons with cash. Result France announced capital controls that included €1,000 cap on cash payments a drop from €3,000. Spain restricts cash payments to £2,500 and Italy restricts them to £1,000.

- J.P. Morgan Chase has put restrictions on borrowers from making cash payments on credit cards, mortgages, equity lines, auto loans and prohibiting the storage of cash in safety deposit boxes.

- Banks in the Euro zone that pay negative interest rates are looking at ways to prevent withdrawals of cash. It raises the question so when is a demand deposit account not a demand deposit account. Banks would not have sufficient cash on hand to cover mass withdrawals. Huge withdrawals to avoid negative interest rates would impact negatively their fractional reserves.

- The Swiss National Bank (SNB) is on record as stating that it doesn't like to see the hoarding of cash to circumvent their negative interest rate policy. Can banks actually refuse to give customers their cash that is legally theirs? It would seem that way.

- A number of banks in Sweden apparently have cashless branches and they refuse to pay out cash. Customers are moving their accounts to banks that will allow them access cash.

- In the US, customers who withdraw $5,000 or more are to be reported. Many banks have also instituted maximum cash withdrawals. Capital controls in the banking system it would seem are becoming normal.

- According to a report HSBC in the UK is interrogating customers on how they earn and spend their money and restricting large cash withdrawals to £5,000.

- The State of Louisiana passed a bill – Bill 195 that would make it easier to track the sales of stolen goods. The bill could have far-reaching consequences in effectively putting every flea market, goodwill, garage sales, Craigslist, and Kijiji out of business. Apparently, the bill requires that second hand goods be paid with credit cards, cheques, money orders, debit cards, or electronic transfer. They no longer can use cash. The bill also required that second hand sellers obtain a considerable amount of information on each buyer. The process seemed to fly in the face that a US dollar is legal tender for all debts.

These examples are merely a few that I have read where cash appears to be under attack. Negative interest rates are not dissimilar to a tax on savings. The use of cash is considered a suspicious activity. Restrictions on the use of cash appears to be becoming more prevalent. In Canada, banks do put restrictions on how much one can withdraw from an ATM. Large withdrawals or deposits come under the auspice of the Financial Transactions and Reports Analysis Centre of Canada (FINTRAC).

Despite using terrorists, jihadists, money launderers and others as an excuse for a cashless society the real target could be the cash underground economy that for the most part can't be monitored or taxed. The size of the Canadian underground economy has been highlighted recently in a report that puts its size at $42.4 billion in 2012 or 2.3% of GDP. A cashless society would be going after everyone to collect taxes from contractors that take cash under the table for renovations to individuals holding Saturday morning garage sales and churches holding rummage sales.

The move to a cashless society is not something that is going to happen overnight. So far, it seems to be being implemented slowly and in stages. Banks, central banks and governments are behind the movement. The technology is already there to move to a cashless society. Eliminating cash allows governments to track everyone both the innocent and the guilty.

The trouble is what impact could the move to a cashless society have on the economy? Already the velocity of money is falling rapidly. In a cashless society, M1 could become a relic of a bygone era. And it could also cause considerable problems as currency to pay for goods and services has been around for centuries and a cashless society might not be fully acceptable by significant portions of the population. The loss of privacy could be only one issue related to a cashless society.

The end of cash could raise more questions than answers. On the surface, it would leave a huge unanswered question as to "what is money worth?" Not much, it seems in a world of negative interest rates and rising bank fees just to place ones money in the bank. Negative interest rates are a distortion of the market as holding cash would be punitive. It could force people into investing in higher risk securities. It could also be good for gold, as gold remains an historical store of value. There is also the law of unintended consequences when one tries to enforce what amounts to what one may call a command economy.

Given that the recent US GDP numbers were quite low and probably negative once one strips out inventory buildup it would not be surprising that the velocity of money (M1 and M2) has fallen further. None of this is positive and it could be another sign that the global economy could be in more trouble then what is currently evident.

Courtesy, David Chapman

CHAPTER 22.

THEY ARE SLOWLY MAKING CASH ILLEGAL

The move to a cashless society won't happen overnight. Instead, it is being implemented very slowly and systematically in a series of incremental steps. All over the planet, governments are starting to place restrictions on the use of cash for security reasons. As citizens, we are being told that this is being done to thwart criminals, terrorists, drug runners, money launderers and tax evaders. Other forms of payment are much easier for governments to track, and so they very much prefer them. But we are rapidly getting to the point where the use of cash is considered to be a "suspicious activity" all by itself.

These days, if you pay a hotel bill with cash or

if you pay for several hundred dollars worth of goods at a store with cash you are probably going to get looked at funny. You see, the truth is that we have already been trained to regard the use of large amounts of cash to be unusual. The next step will be to formally ban large cash transactions like France and other countries in Europe are already doing. Starting in September, cash transactions of more than 1,000 euros will be banned in France. The following comes from a recent Zero Hedge article which detailed what these new restrictions will do…

Prohibiting French residents from making cash payments of more than 1,000 euros, down from the current limit of 3,000 euros.

Given the parlous state of the stagnating French economy the **limit for foreign tourists on currency payments will remain higher, at 10,000 euros down from the current limit of 15,000 euros.**

The threshold below which a French resident is free to convert euros into other currencies **without having to show an identity card** will be slashed from the current level of **8,000 euros to 1,000 euros**.

In addition **any cash deposit or withdrawal of more than 10,000 euros during a single month will be reported to the French anti-fraud and money laundering agency**.

French authorities will also have to be notified of any freight transfers within the EU exceeding 10,000 euros, including checks, pre-paid cards, or **gold**.

Of course Spain has already banned cash transactions of more than 2,500 euros and Italy has already banned cash transactions of more than 1,000 euros.We don't have these kinds of outright bans in the United States just yet, but what we do have are some very strict reporting requirements.For example, if you regularly deposit large amounts of cash, there is a very good chance that you have been the subject of a "suspicious activity report". In 2013, approximately 1.6 million suspicious activity reports were submitted to the federal government.The following guidelines for when a suspicious activity report should be filed come from a government website...*****Banks, bank holding companies, and their subsidiaries are required by federal regulations53 to file a SAR with respect to:

- Criminal violations involving insider abuse in any amount.

- Criminal violations aggregating $5,000 or more when a suspect can be identified.

- Criminal violations aggregating $25,000 or more regardless of a potential suspect.

- Transactions conducted or attempted by, at, or through the bank (or an affiliate) and aggregating $5,000 or more, if the bank or affiliate knows, suspects, or has reason to suspect that the transaction:

- ○ May involve potential money laundering or other illegal activity (e.g., terrorism financing).54

  ○ Is designed to evade the BSA or its implementing regulations.55

  ○ Has no business or apparent lawful purpose or is not the type of transaction that the particular customer would normally be expected to engage in, and the bank knows of no reasonable explanation for the transaction after examining the available facts, including the background and possible purpose of the transaction.

*****Most people don't realize this, but there are minimum quotas for suspicious activity reports that banks must meet. If they do not submit enough suspicious activity reports, they can be fined (or worse).And now the Obama administration is saying that just filling out suspicious activity reports may not be good enough.According to the Wall Street Journal, banks are actually being encouraged to directly contact law enforcement if they see something that does not look right...

The U.S. Justice Department's criminal head said banks may need to go beyond filing suspicious activity reports when they encounter a risky customer.

"The vast majority of financial institutions file suspicious activity reports when they suspect that an account is connected to nefarious activity," said assistant attorney general Leslie Caldwell in a Monday speech, according to prepared remarks. **"But, in appropriate cases, we encourage those institutions to consider whether to take more action: specifically, to alert law enforcement authorities about the problem."**

The remarks indicate that banks may be expected to do more than just file SARs, a responsibility that itself can be expensive and time-consuming.

That should send a chill up your spine.In a recent piece, Simon Black imagined a future scenario in which some unsuspecting American citizen goes to the bank to withdraw a large amount of cash...

Imagine going to the bank to withdraw some cash.

Having some cash on hand is always a prudent strategy, and especially today when more and more bank deposits are creeping into negative territory, meaning that you have to pay the banks for the privilege that they gamble with your money.

You tell the teller that you'd like to withdraw $5,000 from your account. She hesitates nervously and wants to know why.

You try to politely let her know that that's none of the bank's business as it's your money.

The teller disappears for a few minutes, leaving you waiting.

When she returns she tells you that you can collect your money in a few days as they don't have it on hand at the moment.

Slightly irritated because of the inconvenience, you head home.

But as you pull into your driveway later there's an unexpected surprise waiting for you: two police officers would like to have a word with you about your intended withdrawal earlier…

Perhaps you don't think that anything like that could ever happen to you.Well, consider what the feds are doing to one widow in Iowa...

A widow's bank account was seized by the IRS and she now faces **criminal charges** for depositing her legal inheritance money in lumps instead of all together.

Janet Malone, 68, had $18,775 seized from her — money that was legally earned and was legally bestowed to her by her late husband, Ronald Malone. The problem, according to the government, was the fact that she deposited it in several lumps instead of all at once.

According to the Associated Press, Mrs. Malone deposited the cash in increments between $5,800 and $9,000. The widow's private financial affairs evidently set off red flags under the watchful gaze of the federal government.

Remember, she was not guilty of committing any crime other than depositing cash in lumps instead of all at once.If this is how ruthless the feds will be **with an elderly widow**, how would they treat **you** under similar circumstances?So why are they doing this?The truth is that they want to discourage the public from using cash. Our government, just like governments all over the planet, is not being shy about the fact that it does not like cash. If they can make people afraid to use cash, that suits their purposes very well.And with each passing year the restrictions on the use of cash globally will just get tighter and tighter and the role that cash plays in our lives will just become smaller and smaller.In the end, a transition to an almost entirely cashless society will seem almost natural. Cash is being killed off one slow step at a time, and at this point hardly anyone is objecting.

Courtesy, The Economic Collapse

CHAPTER 23.

DOUG CASEY INTERVIEWED BY LOUIS JAMES, EDITOR, INTERNATIONAL SPECULATOR

L: Well, Doug, we've seen another quarter of high volatility and significant world events. What strikes you as most important at present?

Doug: Everything is still held together with chewing gum and baling wire, for which I'm grateful, considering what's coming. It's very clear to me that the global economy is in very much the same space as it was in 2007—in other words, on the edge of a precipice.

[...]

L: On the global economy, my question is

this: If Obama and Yellen have saved the US and Merkel and Draghi are saving the EU, why are commodities selling off so dramatically? Iron, copper, oil—just about everything is selling off. How can an economy be recovering if it's not using raw materials?

Doug: That's another reason why I believe that the Greater Depression started in late 2007. During a depression, people are forced to consume less, and you see that reflected in the price of commodities—at least in real terms. This can be obscured in current price terms, depending on the debasement of the currency in question.

But it's important to remember that commodities are only a good bet when they're cycling upward, and that only lasts for a time. The longest trend of all is the downward trend of real commodities prices, as the march of technology makes them and the cost of life itself cheaper over time. Real commodity prices have been going down for at least 2,000 years, but probably 4,000 or 5,000 years—at least since the invention of agriculture. And I think they will continue falling, despite the fact that most large, high-grade, close-to-surface mineral deposits have been discovered.

L: Hubbert was right about "peak oil" in terms of West Texas Intermediate, but oil is still getting cheaper because of the fracking revolution.

Doug: Exactly. Because we've made so much money on commodities and because we believe in gold and silver as money, people think of us as commodity bulls. But actually, in the big picture, I'm a commodity bear, and always have been. Nanotech will transform city dumps into high-grade ore bodies. The asteroids will be mined at low cost. Ocean water will be processed economically. It's simply a matter of technology and energy. The future could be—should be—better than we can even imagine.

L: I understand that—but I have to step in here and remind readers that gold is not a commodity—or at least not a regular commodity, since it's also the most successful and enduring form of money ever devised.

Doug: Yes. No matter how many times we tell readers that no one can time the market, they still want to know what I think of the timing of the gold market.

So let me tell you that even I have been feeling a bit abused and unloved by the market over the last couple years. If I'm feeling that way, I'm sure the average person in the sector is feeling it in spades—and that's actually a strong sign of a bottom.

It's not as if we're buying at $35 in 1971 or $250 in 2001—both times when gold was clearly a one-way street. But at $1,200, it's very reasonable considering how explosive the world situation is.

L: That's why we call it contrarian investing.

Doug: It's pretty stark. Most of these crappy little mining stocks have no money, no management, no assets. In bull markets, they're still crappy companies, but they can raise money, drill some holes in the ground, and hope to get lucky. But now they're turning into shells, and that's another sign of a resource sector bottom.

On the other hand, Wall Street has been rising for about seven years now, which is record territory. Several major indices have hit new records. These are signs of a market top. If the market collapses, it can take everything down with it. Mining stocks are also stocks.

L: What about earnings? Don't higher Es justify higher Ps?

Doug: They do, but earnings can be pumped up by things like sacrificing sustaining capital to maximize near-term profit or buying back shares instead of investing in new growth. As per your question about commodities, I don't believe the real economy is truly in recovery, and I don't believe the earnings we've seen are sustainable; I expect them to collapse.

That in turn could produce a general stock market crash as happened in 1929 and on into the 1930s. The odds are overwhelming that that's going to happen to the bond market, and if the bond market crashes, that's going to devastate the stock market, which will in turn bring down the real estate market.

L: There you go again, Mr. Sunshine.

Doug: You know I'm not trying to be perverse—that's just the way the world is.

L: So what does that leave?

Doug: Most people would say cash, but as we've seen in the last few years, every government in the world—including the US and EU—is more than willing to print unbelievable amounts of money to try to paper their problems over. That's going to go into hyper-drive in the next round, trashing the value of currencies around the world as it does.

L: But gold is the real cash of the world—always has been.

Doug: Yes. We can't stress enough that the primary reason for owning gold today isn't to speculate on its price rising, but for prudence, for wealth preservation. For speculation, that's what gold stocks are for, especially the kind you follow in the *International Speculator*.

The good thing about all the money printing is that we can predict that it will create more bubbles. Hopefully these stocks will be among the bubbles.

Currencies come and go, but over the centuries, gold has always held value. About 100 years ago, you could buy a good suit with an ounce of gold, and that's still true today—and I expect it will still be true for the foreseeable future.

In fact, as unlikely as it may seem to mainstream economic thinkers today, one of the more likely outcomes of the financial turmoil ahead is that some country or another is going to reinstitute the gold standard.

We don't need a gold standard, of course, or any currencies at all, for that matter. People just need to be free to own and trade in gold. Period. Today, it can be represented by computer bits on your iPhone, of course.

I think it will probably start with China or Russia, or possibly an Islamic country serious about its interpretation of the Koran. You know that the Prophet, peace be upon him, said in the Koran—which everyone knows is the direct and incontrovertible word of Allah himself—that one should only use the dirham and dinar as money. These are units of silver and gold.

L: There have been attempts, but none has gotten very far.

Doug: The new ISIS caliphate says it will operate according to the Koran on all matters, including money. They may make it stick, at least in the lands over which they have sway. Whatever else one might say about them, you have to admit they really are sincere fanatics. If someone says they believe something and they actually try to do what they say they believe, that's worthy of some respect, even if you don't share those beliefs. They appear to be not just talking the talk, but walking the walk, in every respect.

L: Just the same, Doug, I wouldn't go pay my respects in person, if I were you.

Doug: No question. They are clearly... unpleasant people. I'm certain I'd end up in one of those orange jumpsuits if I did go back to Syria or Iraq, and I doubt they'd consider my opinion over whether to behead me or burn me alive in a cage. But that's got nothing to do with the fact that they appear to be trying to act consistently with their principles, and it's intellectually dishonest to dismiss that.

L: Well, I'd hate to see gold branded as "the preferred money of theocratic fanatics," but I do understand your intellectual point. Your remarks about evidence of a bottom are encouraging. I've heard it said by veteran investors with more experience than I have that the kind of bumping along the bottom we've been suffering through is actually a classic sign of a bottom in a long cycle. Do you agree?

Doug: Yes, I do. I still think that intraday low

of around $1,140 last November was likely the actual bottom.

L: Personally, I was very encouraged then, because gold had broken below its December 2013 low, and it seemed that every pundit and blogger in the world was saying that there was nothing to stop the fall short of $1,000, or even $700. It was widely believed that breaching the prior low was the trigger that would take it much lower—but that's not what happened. Instead, the new low was a buying signal to Russians, Chinese, Indians, and others, and gold shot right back up again.

Doug: Agreed. In absolute terms, gold isn't as good a value as it was in 2001, when I was telling readers that if I could call their brokers and buy gold for them, I would. On the other hand, the world is far, far less stable, so the prudence of owning precious metals is more paramount than ever.

You've got to own gold, because as we've often pointed out, it's the only financial asset that is not simultaneously someone else's liability. That's particularly so when you remember that in reality, all of the major banks of the world are bankrupt. Between the fractional reserve system and the preponderance of bad loans and other factors, there isn't a one of them I'd trust.

Worse, if you have a lot of money in a bank, you may think it's an asset, but the bank thinks it's a liability, and it's subject to seizure, come the bail-ins such as we saw in Cyprus. The EU is already laying the groundwork for that.

Courtesy, Doug Casey, International Speculator

CHAPTER 24.

OBAMA CONTINUES TO BE HUMILIATED BY THE RISING ANTI-DOLLAR ALLIANCE

Now it's Austria, Switzerland, and Australia that have joined dozens of other countries around the world in the anti-dollar alliance.These nations, which also include most US 'allies' in Western Europe like Germany, France and the UK, have all signed on to be founding members of China's new Asia Infrastructure Investment Bank (AIIB).The AIIB is the biggest disruption to the global monetary system since the end of World War II.For decades, global finance has been completely dominated by the United States... and the US dollar.

This is the reason why a transaction for oil

between Bangladesh and Brazil will close and settle in US dollars. It's why a French aircraft manufacturer will sell its jets to European airlines... not in euros, but in US dollars. It's why a contract for aluminum traded in London will clear in US dollars.Nearly every major financial or commodity contract in the world is priced in US dollars. And this requires that the entire world not only holds US dollars in order to engage in trade, but to also use the US banking system.

This has put the United States in a position of unparalleled privilege.Think about it—the rest of the world placed its trust and confidence in the US banking system, the US government, and the US dollar. And in return, this privilege has afforded the United States the opportunity to indebt itself more than any other nation in the history of the world, quintuple its money supply, and wage endless wars overseas... all with relatively minor consequences.

But here's the thing: the US has been

conspicuously abusing this privilege for years. They've taken things too far. Debt levels are so obscene it's now almost mathematically impossible for the US to ever pay it off. The US banking system led the world into the greatest financial crisis it had seen since the Great Depression. The US government now even brazenly spies on its own allies. This isn't how you maintain the trust and confidence of the rest of the world.

Nearly every other nation out there has had enough. And they're locking arms with China's new AIIB in a clear sign of alignment against the US government and the US dollar. What's really incredible is how China was able to convince European nations to join AIIB.

Unlike, say, the World Bank, which is totally dominated by the United States, China freely gave up veto power in AIIB... showing willingness to SHARE POWER with other nations. This is something that the United States government has never been willing to do.

Of course, the Obama administration has vigorously protested this move by its allies and has gone on the offensive to discredit the AIIB. As US Treasury Secretary Jacob Lew told Congress last week, "Our concern has always been—will [AIIB] adhere to the kinds of high standards that the international financial institutions developed..." Yeah right... because the US financial system upholds such high standards of international finance. What a farce. (Lew also told Congress that "[o]ur international credibility and influence are being threatened..." File that one under 'no shit, Sherlock.')

And yet, despite all the grumbling from the United States, allies are still jumping into bed with China. Even CANADA is now 'considering' joining AIIB. Now with its back against the wall, the US is finally starting to acknowledge reality… suggesting that it might possibly be willing to 'work with' the AIIB. It's embarrassing, really…

To paraphrase Gandhi in this context: The US first ignored China's rise and AIIB. Then they laughed at it. Then it tried to fight it. And then China won.

Courtesy, SovereignMan.com

CHAPTER 25.

CONCLUSION AND RECOMMENDATIONS

It has been almost two years since we wrote THE COMING BANKING HOLIDAY, and appeared on numerous radio talk shows promoting the book, but more importantly alerting Americans to the dangers we all now face. <u>Will we face a banking holiday as predicted by Gerald Celente, similar to the FDR style of 1933, and outlined in our first book?</u>

It doesn't appear that we will, as we first thought in the original book. It *will occur* however, but in a subtler, less radical form. Ever since the repeal of the Glass-Steagall Act of 1933, by the Clinton administration, the U.S. banking system has never been the same.

What the repeal of the act did was to permit banks to borrow money at almost zero interest rates, and recklessly gamble with it, and our money. Up until November 16 of 2014, it was the taxpayers money that was on the line, should a bank fail (called a *bail out*). After November 16th, if any of the G-20 banks around the world fail, it would the *depositors* that would be *"bailing out"* the banks. This newly adopted protocol (now called *bail in*) is now essentially the law of the land in the U.S., although Congress has not approved it, nor was any treaty signed.

What has us so concerned us, is that most of us hold our savings and checking in one of the top six U.S. banks. And, every one of them are technically insolvent. For example, if The Bank Of America is pulled under by it's Merrill Lynch subsidiary holding 50 trillion in derivatives, its their *depositors* that would have to step in, and *save the day*. The FDIC would be called in to oversee the bankruptcy proceedings, and tally up the deposits and commodity derivatives on the balance sheet. Since the derivatives are calculated first, in all likelihood, there would be zero net assets for the FDIC to work with.

The FDIC would then have to attempt to borrow perhaps trillions of dollars from the U.S. Treasury to pay off the bank depositors with assets under $250,000. With derivatives involved, it is likely that even the U.S. Treasury would not be able to pay off the anticipated trillions at stake.

Another concern of ours... if the Bank of America were to go under, it's thought that *a domino effect* would occur (again, due to the magnitude of derivatives). Thus, it is reasonable to predict that if just *one* of the six major banks were to go under, the other five would soon follow. This would make it virtually impossible for the FDIC to work out a solution.

During the entire sorting-out process, which could take as long as fifteen years, *depositor's accounts would be frozen*. The depositor would be unable to pay their mortgage, food bill, or any bill for that matter. Not only would the depositor be without funds, but thousands of businesses having accounts at these six large banks, would have their working capital frozen, and soon be out of business.

When this banking fiasco reaches crisis proportions, the Federal Reserve, will have to step in. Printing money on such a scale that would be necessary, would surely sink the U.S. dollar. The only choice that the Fed would have, would be to proceed with a plan to implement *an electronic digital currency,* much like credit cards are used today. This could be the subject of a subsequent book.

Now here's the wildcard! As we write this book, May 6, 2015, the **Trans Pacific Partnership** legislation has not yet been approved by Congress. It has been fast-tracked and approved by a Senate committee however. If finally approved by congress, and it appears that it will be, since Congress has no idea what's in it (as it's secret), this could change everything. Assuming the bill will be passed, and put into law, the TPP committee, made up of a few highly paid international attorneys, could rule against the recent "bail in" measure approved by the G-20 group.

Therefore, if The Bank Of America did go under, the TPP could rule that "Bail ins" would not apply in this case, as it would affect the shareholders of the corporation (Bank Of America). What a crazy world we now live in. We will discuss the TPP and it's affect on our new "Bail In" policies in our monthly newsletters. This is big news!

However, the purpose of *this* book, is to point out to the reader, the danger present in today's savings and checking accounts. The FDIC will probably not be able to live up to it's $250,000 guarantee. And, even if it could by using an electronic currency, or a currency based on a basket of world currencies, the implementation time-period (to correct this mess) would be unacceptable. Americans cannot wait fifteen years, or that matter, even a few months, to get at their money. To survive they have to access to at least *some* funds immediately.

So what to do? In all our books, we try to present the problem, present essays that discuss the problem, and then recommend what we feel may be a reasonable solution.

Here's what Monica and I recommend you do now:

- *First of all get your checking, savings, and business accounts out of the large U.S. major banks immediately. Open up a bank account at a small, local, well-capitalized U.S. bank.* Keep only enough cash in the account(s) to pay your bills, and take care of small emergencies.

- *Then, open a custodian-type savings account* in New Zealand, or Australia. Their banks are solvent, and among the strongest in the world. Their governments have little or no debt. By opening a savings account with a *custodian firm,* such as *Aegis, Ltd.,* the largest custodian in NZ, you will get added protection. They only hold the strongest Bank's CD's in trust for you. Their NZ & Australian bank CD's are short term, only a month in duration. They roll over each month at a high competitive interest rate. We mention this, as if you need to wire funds to your U.S. bank, you need only wait a few days, not months. The key is to get *some* of your savings dollars out of the U.S., and over to another first world country. *We'd be glad to e-mail you information on how to open an account with Aegis, Ltd.*

- ***Open up a stock brokerage account*** with a firm that does *not* deal with derivatives. We chose Interactive Brokers for that reason, and have been with them for many years. It is recommended that you now be in 100% cash (in U.S. dollars). Then when our advisers give us the signal, go into quality mining stocks. At that point, also start to invest in large industrial companies that have substance (real wealth). E-mail us to get on our complimentary newsletter which will tell you when to begin investing in the markets. *If you'd like to join us at Interactive Brokers, and piggy-back on our investment selections, we'd be glad to have you with us; just let us know (wallst101@hotmail.com).* We feel that the deflation cycle has to play out for a few more months, stocks drop sharply, and then rise to new heights. At Interactive

Brokers, we use the *Gold Stock Analyst* method of John Doody, to make our stock selections. John's program has increased 924% from 2001 to mid 2014. We even wrote a book about it called: *THE COMING GOLD & SILVER SHARE EXPLOSION!*. It's out now in paperback (Amazon), Kindle, and soon to be on *Audible*.

Thanks for purchasing this, our sixth book! We wish you the best in getting through this new financial crisis. Please keep e-mailing us your questions, and requested topics for future books.

John & Monica

www.ingramcontent.com/pod-product-compliance
Lightning Source LLC
Chambersburg PA
CBHW072302200526
45168CB00014B/212